PRISON:

Getting Out by Going In

Freedom Before Release

Getting Out

By Going In ™

If you are in prison and reading this, it is likely this book was provided to you as a gift, a donation from someone who cares about your internal freedom.

It may be a gift from a friend, a family member, an inmate, a family member of an inmate, an ex-offender, or a freeman who knows your struggle.

The point is....

you are not alone in your journey. Someone cares about you and wants you to be internally free.

Change Your Luck by Changing Your Mindset.
You may use the tools described in this book to widen your
options and change your luck... it's up to you.

What incarcerated youth have said about the GOGI techniques described in this book...

"I learned how to control my anger a little bit more than I usually could...and when I get out I am going to go to school and college and major in real-estate, also stay away from the bad and go with the good."
- H. L. GOGI graduate

"I learned that being mad at myself or at other people is not the answer."
- J. R. GOGI graduate

"I learned how to talk to staff and to follow the rules better."
- K. T. GOGI graduate

"I have become a much more patient person. I am able to relax and ease tension."
- D. S. GOGI graduate

"I learned that I should control my anger when I come face to face with a real problem."
- A. A. GOGI graduate

"I used to have a short temper and [now] whenever I get angry, I just remember what she taught me then and I relax myself."
- B. W. GOGI graduate

"I have learned how to work, how to set goals, and how to express myself."
- V. T. GOGI graduate

**What inmates have said about the
GOGI techniques described in this book...**

*"After feeling like I was the living dead over the past eight years
you gave me the tools that brought me back to life. This
gladiator school turned into a big think tank for me and
time is flying by. I'm happy to say that I'll finally be
going home next month, but with a new way of living.
My relationship with my children, my parents,
and myself has put me in control of my life, made
me more focused and put me in a state of mind
that can conquer any goal that I set."*
- D. F. GOGI graduate

*"The course helps me everyday and long term
I'll be able to use these techniques indefinitely."*
- H. L. GOGI graduate

*"I have used some communication techniques I learned with
my wife and I plan to use them when I get out. Most inmates
are in prison not only physically but mentally too.
This class would help those free themselves, in order for them
to grow, retain and reprogram their reactions."*
- V. N. GOGI graduate

*"This course is important for not only inmates, but free
people. I've learned that my breathing, posture, and
thinking will help me with everyday problem solving."*
- D. V. GOGI graduate

ISBN-10: 0-9786721-0-0
ISBN-13: 978-0-9786721-0-2

Disclaimer
This book and information contained herein is for educational and inspirational purposes only and not to be used for self-treatment. Likewise, information contained herein is not intended or implied to be a substitute for professional medical advice or a replacement for any treatment. Always seek the advice of your physician or other qualified health provider for all medical problems, treatments, or with any questions you may have regarding a medical condition.

© Cover, Logo, Images courtesy of Getting Out by Going In
Cover Design: Catherine Brankov
Cover Art and Illustrations: Jabriel Parks
Layout: Roselle Kipp

For questions, e-mail <info@gettingoutbygoingin.org> or write to:
GETTING OUT BY GOING IN, PO Box 88969, Los Angeles, CA, 90009, USA

Published in the United States of America by Lightning Source, Inc.

Print is last number listed: 9 8 7 6 5 4 3

PRISON:

Getting Out by Going In

Freedom Before Release

By COACH MARA LEIGH TAYLOR

Comments by DeJuan Verrett
Foreword by Bo Lozoff

Getting Out
GO
By Going In ™

2202 RAYBURN HOUSE OFFICE BUILDING
WASHINGTON, DC 20515-0539
(202) 225-4111
FAX: (202) 226-0335

305 NORTH HARBOR BOULEVARD
SUITE 300
FULLERTON, CALIFORNIA 92832
(714) 992-8081
(562) 220-2411
FAX: (714) 992-1668

UNITED STATES
HOUSE OF REPRESENTATIVES

INTERNATIONAL RELATIONS
Subcommittees:
Chairman, International Terrorism
and Nonproliferation
Vice Chairman, Africa, Global Human Rights,
and International Operations
Oversight and Investigations

FINANCIAL SERVICES
Subcommittees:
Capital Markets, Insurance and
Government Sponsored Enterprises
Financial Institutions and
Consumer Credit
Oversight and Investigations

EDWARD R. ROYCE
Fortieth District-California

March 21, 2006

Ms. Mara Leigh Taylor
Getting Out By Going In

Dear Ms. Taylor:

I am pleased to express my strong and earnest support for your organization, Getting Out by Going In (GOGI). GOGI has proven itself as a key component for reducing crime and relieving the recidivism crisis in California for more than four years with more than 500 graduates thus far, and I congratulate you on this achievement.

Moreover, since California has the largest state prison expenditure in the U.S. at 4.2 billion dollars per year, GOGI's effort to relieve the recidivism is influential in providing the opportunity to redirect our State's growing corrections budget into other programs such as health, education and natural resources. In federal prisons throughout California, the GOGI curriculum has proven very successful and has therefore become a component of the mandated release preparation curriculum, the drug treatment curriculum and anger management curriculum.

I applaud your mission to positively affect more than one million lives by 2010 and am aware that you are applying for several federal grants. I strongly urge each granting agency to give your application their prompt and most careful consideration. If any federal departments or agencies have any questions, please do not hesitate to have them contact me at my district office.

Sincerely,

EDWARD R. ROYCE

Foreword
by Bo Lozoff

Sita and Bo Lozoff

Many people ask me why I work in such brutal, negative environments as prisons. They say "Gee, it must be really depressing." I'm sure Coach Taylor hears the same remarks about her work.

While it is certainly true that prisons are brutal and negative environments, how can it be depressing to witness people making sensational leaps and bounds on their life journeys, their spiritual journeys? For some mysterious reason, we human beings sometimes reveal our brightest, most beautiful nature when we are faced with great adversity.

For those of us who do this kind of work in prisons,

Bo and Sita Lozoff pictured with the volunteers and staff of the Prison-Ashram Project in North Carolina.

the process of profound transformation that occurs in people like DeJuan Verrett, one of the contributors to this book who served sixteen years behind bars, is nothing short of miraculous, amazing, and inspiring to watch. It's a privilege of the highest order and a reminder that no matter what we have done in the past, so long as we still draw breath, we are capable of the very best change possible for a human being. You and I

Sita in the HKF offices.

are supposed to know it is never our prerogative to give up on anyone's transformation. You and I are supposed to know it is never our prerogative to give up on anyone's transformation

Bo and his "grandchildren."

When Jesus chose Saul of Tarsus – a man as evil and despicable as Charles Manson or Timothy McVeigh or anyone else we love to demonize – to transform into Saint Paul, wasn't He expressly reminding us that anyone, any lowlife killer or thug, still bears the seeds of sainthood in his heart of hearts? Why else would He choose Saul – merely bad taste? No, He chose Saul to humble us and make it clear that it is never too late for a sinner to become a saint.

Unfortunately our society seems to have lost sight of this principle, and we seem very quick to give up on people who commit crimes. More and more we even give up on juvenile offenders by trying them as adults and sentencing them to life without parole.

Yes, this is certainly a brutal and negative backdrop for the kind of work that some of us do with prisoners. But what happens against this terrible backdrop is nothing short of astonishing. With just the slightest sincere help, men and women face themselves honestly, they accept responsibility for their lives and their choices, they open their hearts to true humility and compassion more deeply than most of the "freeworlders" who sentenced them to prison, and they become some of the finest people one could ever meet.

My own Prison-Ashram Project has been encouraging and witnessing such transformation for many years, and now

Coach Taylor's work, especially through her program "Getting Out by Going In," is following the same cues and witnessing the same results. Coach Taylor's background and methodologies come more from a psychological perspective because that is

Bo working the HKF land in Mebane, North Carolina.

her training, but her psychological work is firmly grounded in the same simple spiritual principles that propel my own. She understands that "talk is cheap." She knows that change must come from practical shifts in body, mind and spirit. And her methods work with each one of those areas.

Coach Taylor and her program believe in the worth and integrity of each individual. And she knows it takes a lot of hard work to change lifelong patterns and habits/ Her program is realistic and requires accountability. It is not just a "feel-good" strategy for coping with prison life. It is about change, about transformation, about becoming different than we once were, becoming freer and kinder and more responsive to life's ups and downs in productive ways rather than destructive ways.

It's interesting to see that the title of my first book, "We're All Doing Time," and the title of this program,

Bo Lozoff and friend
Coach Taylor

"Getting Out by Going In," are saying the same things from two opposite directions. My title implies that even we who are not behind bars are doing time in the prisons of our minds and habits. And Coach Taylor's title reminds us that those of us who ARE behind bars can become free long before the iron gates open to release our bodies. Same thing. We're indeed all doing time, and we can all indeed become free by turning inward and facing the truths of our existence.

If this book and program seem to speak to your situation, I encourage you to deal with the insights and practices it offers with all your heart. We really can change more than you may ever have allowed yourself to dream....

Bo Lozoff
September 2006

The popular book, "We're All Doing Time," written by Bo Lozoff, is considered to be the "Bible for Incarceration," by many inmates and is both inspirational and hopeful. In their work, Bo and Sita offer inspirational and insightful materials for incarcerated individuals. You may request Bo's writings or his music by sending a note to Sita and Bo at: Human Kindness Foundation, PO Box 61619, Durham, NC 27715 USA.

A lazy fall day on the HKF land in North Carolina. As you read the pages of this book, relax and imagine yourself swinging on a hammock enjoying the stillness and peace offered.

THIS BOOK WAS CREATED FOR YOU.
IT WAS DESIGNED TO HELP SET YOU FREE.

*The GOGI objective is that you will find inspiration
from the information provided in this book through the
ideas, tools, thoughts, examples, and testimonials.
The GOGI goal is that in reading and learning the material
herein you will find INTERNAL FREEDOM now and forever.*

I invite you to sincerely explore...
1) Read the words.
2) Practice the tools.
3) Give attention to the examples.
4) Read and relate to the testimonials.

*Internal freedom is a journey for every human.
Within these pages you may find the opportunity to discover the
hidden secret.*

Freedom, true freedom, is always internal.

*GETTING OUT of internal prison requires that you start
GOING IN for your answers.*

Coach Taylor

Personal Tools for Internal Freedom Help you to. . .

LET GO, FORGIVE & CLAIM RESPONSIBILITY

BOSS OF YOUR BRAIN allows you to take control of all your thoughts and actions.

BELLY BREATHING allows you to take control of your entire body.

FIVE SECOND LIGHTSWITCH allows you to stop and think before you act.

WHAT IF? allows you to think from a powerful and positive perspective.

POSITIVE TWA
(Thoughts, Words, Actions)
TWA are three keys that allows you to control your thoughts, word, and actions.

REALITY CHECK allows you to accept the natural process of change.

Ideas to make your life more powerful...

Words from a brother...

Coach DJ by Jabriel Parks

On the 8th day of May, 2006, DeJuan Verrett was released from 16 years in Federal Corrections Institutions. But he was a free man long before the key was turned and he returned to his home town of San Pedro, California.

He began the journey inward toward freedom behind the wall. He continues the journey inward. DJ is a certified "Coach" for the California based Non-Profit organization dedicated to incarcerated and at-risk individuals and appropriately named GETTING OUT BY GOING IN.

Coach DJ helps empower incarcerated and at-risk individuals. He volunteers his time as a speaker and teacher of the GOGI concepts for lasting change.

Coach DJ's "Words from a brother" comments are interspersed throughout this book and offer insight that only comes from his experiences.

Words from a brother...

My name is DeJuan Lamonte Verrett. My retired BOP number is 92857-012. This number will not be hung on any rafter. It will be burned, forgotten about because I am not a number. I am a spiritual being who has had trying human experiences.

I thought I was in control of my life but my actions led me to a negative human experience which delivered me to the Bureau of Prisons for 16 years, 3 months and 2 days. I fought that feeling that I was a spiritual being, for the majority of my life; and for the majority of my incarceration. But one day, I felt different.

One day I felt the difference between positive influence and negative influence. I had only encouraged people in a negative way. I helped create or added to unsafe community, and irresponsible actions. I apologize to my community, to my family, to myself for the negativity. Now I am compelled to influence my family, my community and myself in a positive way. Hopefully I can influence you, too.

I thought because the way I lived in the streets, the prestige that I had, that I was better than everyone else. But now, all I want to be is better than I was. This is why I am adding my two cents to this book through my experiences and information I was given.

Man. For all you cats that's behind the wall, there is hope. But you have to want it. I know that some of who you might read this book and your release date might be next year or a few years down the line or you might not ever come home.

Continued on next page

I have to give you the real. You can free yourself under any circumstance. But I cannot free you. I can show you what I have done, but you have to sincerely honestly practice to free yourself.

And then one day you will remember your partna's words and say, "the homie gave me the road map to spiritual freedom because it was given to him freely." Remember, practice makes perfect.

In closing, holla at your boy. Peace.

GOGI Coach DJ
Getting Out By Going In
PO Box 88969
Los Angeles, CA 90009
USA

The People of GOGI

Coach Alex, Coach DJ, Coach Alma and Coach Estefania at a GOGI coach graduation in 2006.

TABLE OF CONTENTS

Are There Good Guys In Prison?

By Coach Taylor

Coach Taylor by Jabriel Parks

I ask myself almost every day if the events that unfold in my life are more under my control than I like to admit.

I ask myself, "Why am I imprisoned by situations, and circumstances, and duties, and obligations, and rules, and restrictions, and expectations?" Whose life am I living?

Why has your life turned out the way it is right now? Was there something that you could have done differently to get a different set of results in your life? Ask yourself one simple question, "Am I really living my life, or is my life living me?"

To be honest with you, MY LIFE LIVES ME most of the time. I struggle each and every day to maintain internal freedom. I must continually remind myself that I control my thoughts and reactions. I must remind myself that if I am in prison, it is a prison of my own making. Only I have the key to my internal freedom.

This personal quest for internal freedom is what has drawn me to a prison ministry and prison volunteer work. I am searching for my own internal freedom. I am attempting to GET OUT of my personal prison by GOING IN. In a very real sense, my prison walls might be just as thick as yours.

I am comfortable when I enter a setting like incarceration because the thick walls and barbed wires are

familiar. They are an externalization of an internal prison of which I have suffered for a very long time.

My own prison walls are just as real to me and, at times, just as discouraging.

Through my volunteer work with the "physically imprisoned," I have experienced the

Coach Taylor with artwork given to GOGI from a prisoner serving a life sentence in Romania.

rewarding insights and perceptual shifts, which have removed the bricks – one by one – and permitted my internal freedom.

Through my volunteer work with inmates, I have come to realize that experiences in prison can be painful if we permit them to be that way. And, within the walls of all prisons, we might also find internal freedom, if we permit that journey.

Through my work, I have also come to realize that most people are not inherently bad, nor do they intentionally behave badly. If given the choice of a legit career or a career constantly teetering on the brink of incarceration, the answer is obvious *for most individuals. I believe that people may resort to bad behavior when they lack information, opportunity and support. Bad behavior is a choice of an individual.*

Yet, bad behavior, does not define the individual. Bad behavior describes the choice of the individual. Bad behavior is simply bad behavior — a choice that can be unchosen.

Also, good behavior does not define the individual and is a choice. Good behavior defines the behavioral choice of the individual.

Furthermore, I believe that anyone can choose good behavior.

There are no bad people, just "bad" or "unacceptable" choices made by individual. And, all individuals can choose bad or good behavior.

Coach Taylor as a guest speaker to university psychology students in Romania.

I believe at any time in our lives we can change our choices. I believe at any time in our lives we can change our thoughts. I also believe at any time in our lives we can change our responses.

To do this, most of us need adequate and sustained help in our efforts to make lasting changes. Hopefully, my words will provide a little sustained help in your personal effort to implement change in your life.

Within the United States, most State and Federal prisons permit qualified volunteer programs for the continuing education and "rehabilitation" of their population. The development of the 6-week GOGI (pronounced Go-Gee like Yogi Bear) curriculum was inspired by volunteer participation of more than 500 incarcerated individuals from 2003 to 2006.

As heavy metal doors slam behind me each time I am permitted access to enter a teaching environment with prisoners, I am reminded of my personal imprisonment and of my personal journey inward for answers. I am thankful for the opportunity to journey inward from behind the wall.

Coach Taylor

GETTING OUT BY GOING IN is a non-profit organization based in California. GOGI is dedicated to helping

people make positive life choices.

To participate, even in a small way, in your release from life's internal prison is a joy beyond measure. I cannot help but be inspired by the possibilities awaiting us all.

What if inmates were better off after their release from prison — because of their experiences in a prison facility?

What if they were welcomed into society for the insight that they could provide to at-risk and incarcerated individuals? What if the setting of incarceration was a place to learn core human values of personal and professional growth and spiritual exploration?

What if it was an institution of "Higher Learning" where the importance of kindness, honesty and goodwill was of paramount importance?

What if the core human concepts of integrity, honor, devotion and personal responsibility were highly regarded in education, as well as in the incarceration environment?

What if we all took the journey inward?

The People of GOGI

Coach Taylor with GOGI graduate, "Wally."

The possibilities of internal freedom are endless. They begin with you, the reader.

Your Freedom is dependent upon your willingness to journey inward. It is never too late or too difficult to take that first step toward internal freedom.

Coach Taylor
Founder / President
GETTING OUT BY GOING IN

There are many ways to make changes in your life. Listed below are some tips from other readers. Set your own pace. You can make certain that the changes you WANT to make -- are the changes that you actually make happen!

1) Read this book (and all books, for that matter) with a pencil nearby. Write thoughts that you have in the margins of the book. Writing helps the brain remember things. Don't worry, unlike what school teachers taught, it's OK, in fact it is good learning to write in a book you own.

2) When you finish each chapter set the book down. Write a letter to someone sharing what you have learned in that chapter. If you don't write letters then write down notes for yourself about the chapter. Thinking, pondering and writing gets the information into your brain cells forever.

3) Reread the chapter again to see what you might have missed on the first reading. This provides even deeper learning.

4) Once you have read the entire book, open it up again and start from the beginning and reread every word. Layers of skills and talents are built with repetition.

5) Observe others who display natural skills with the tools described. Watch what they do, what they say.

6) Share the ideas on telephone calls or on visits with family, children, and friends. Teaching is the final step in learning.

7) Finally, share or give the book to someone. Help teach them how you applied the tools in your life. Giving is the acknowledgement of completion.

CHAPTER ONE
RELEASE PREPARATION

Freedom Awaits You...

Welcome to the journey of getting out of your prison before your release from physical confinement. Experiencing internal freedom is possible for any imprisoned individual, irrespective of the walls defining the physical confinement.

Whether your prison is a State penitentiary, a Bureau of Prisons (BOP) facility, a dead-end job, an economic hardship, a bad marriage, a disabled body, or an addiction - it is possible for you to create the unique experience of internal freedom. You can "get out" of the habits and decision-making ruts that may have led to your time behind bars.

What is available to you during "lock-up" is an unlimited potential for internal freedom. You are able to internalize changes without the chaos of life or the limits that were created by habits and behaviors which hamper your progress.

No one wants to be behind bars. Confinement provides an opportunity to focus and dramatically change your life by doing things differently — even if you might be told how to dress, how and where to stand, or even how and why to walk.

The powerful truth, however, is that **no one, absolutely no one** can tell you what or how to think. No one can limit your internal freedom.

How you think *is* your personal journey toward internal freedom. How you think *is* your set of keys out of prison. While incarcerated you have the opportunity to master, if you will, the fine art of internal freedom.

> *It is a joy to be hidden but disaster not to be found.*
> *D. W. Winnicott*
> *Psychologist*

What if you imagined your incarceration as a college or a scientific laboratory for you to experiment with your own internal change? This laboratory would afford you increasing amounts of freedom with every step you take inward to your own soul's strength, goodness and intelligence.

You have the opportunity to experiment, test, learn, and grow while behind bars and ultimately free yourself. **Internal freedom is available to everyone**, even if very few actually make it their priority.

The internal journey towards internal freedom requires focus and dedication. It takes time and effort, and is oftentimes absent immediate gratification. It can be a lonely trail, testing your internal fortitude beyond all reasonable bounds.

Many free people live and die in prison, limited by fear, anger, resentment and blame others for their own plight. You have a unique opportunity to walk beyond these walls and find internal freedom.

Author and inmate advocate, Bo Lozoff, has been reaching out to inmates for more than three decades. He authored the popular book, "We're All Doing Time," as well as other inspiring and insightful books.

He describes the journey of incarceration in a way that may be helpful for you. In his view, incarceration is similar to being tossed off the train of society. An inmate may roll down a dusty bank into the desert, and be discarded without a second thought.

The fact is, that the train of society that Bo describes is a pending train wreck of consumerism — where the quest for *more*, *faster*, *better* and *bigger* eats up the soul of man.

Yet, perhaps your life can truly begin by turning inward for freedom in an effort to spare yourself from feeling like you have been tossed off society's train.

Much of the material explored in "PRISON: GETTING OUT BY GOING IN," reflects the spiritual concepts discussed in Bo Lozoff's work with inmates.

To a large extent, the material that GOGI offers is consistent with religious and spiritual practices that are universally empowering for practitioners.

> *A torrent of forces works against successful reentry of the incarcerated individual and yet, sometimes all a person needs is a roadmap with information, support and opportunity. The tools contained in this study course are intended to provide that roadmap.*
>
> *Coach Taylor*

Most importantly is the simple fact that the material in this book provides practical tools. They may enable you to put basic spiritual concepts and self-improvement concepts into **action for yourself**.

These concepts and tools represent portions of the GOGI course curriculum designed for the incarcerated individual. They combine an overview of the body's physiological operation (BODY), the mind's complex simplicity (MIND) and the human spirit's resiliency (SPIRIT).

The material provides assistance for you to gain internal freedom during your everyday experiences behind bars. It is also likely that this information can increase your success after your release.

In other words, you can choose to utilize these tools to create a powerfully successful, happy life for yourself, regardless of where you lay your head at night.

Change is an individual process. Change cannot be forced upon the inmate, nor can it be mandated as a release requirement. Internal change is possible during incarceration but is not a guarantee of the process.

Here is what Coach DJ has to say on the subject:

Words from a brother...
External change starts with internal change. You have to be open and willing to do the work. Me, I did not have the tools, the information or the avenues for this, but I knew it was inside of me. I didn't know how to bring it out.

I've learned some of the techniques because Coach Taylor brought the information. Before I came to the GETTING OUT BY GOING IN program, I knew I was supposed to do something else with my life. I ignored that inner feeling with drugs and alcohol, even in the prison setting. I made my wine. I did all that. Caught up with the prison life.

One day, every-thing changed. I got tired of fighting. The internal voice inside me was getting greater and greater.

I finally submitted to it. Once I submitted to it, I became willing to receive the information and the information was given to me freely.

The Five Second Lightswitch, and Belly Breathing, taking a deep breath so I can feel who I am.

Now I have the information of "fight of flight" and the limbic system of my brain.

Once I got these tools, I applied them. But it only works if you work it. I practice on a daily basis. Once I practiced on a daily basis, I started feeling different.

Like I used to say, "nothing is special about me," but with internal change I recognized that something IS special about me. My life has become possible from my willingness, my intentions.

With that right there - willingness and my intentions - I do have to thank God first for giving me courage.

It might sound crazy to you, but I had to go to prison because I was doing my will. Now that I am open and free, I am adding my two cents to this chapter of finding internal peace and tranquility.

I am living proof that it does work. These are just words from a brother. Peace.

The People of GOGI

Coach Cathleen after a day volunteering with GOGI youth.

THE CONTRIBUTION OF CLINICAL PSYCHOLOGY

Several clinical psychology modalities were used in the formulation of techniques used in this material

While psychologically based, the techniques in the GOGI curriculum are simple, understandable and organic to the individual experience.

The techniques are uniquely combined but not in a "secret combination." Some prefer scientific evidence, a religious foundation, or to see the tools in action. Some only get motivated to change by reading comments from a brother. Individuals pick and choose what fits their particular style of learning.

The RapidChange Therapy (RCT) methodology used in developing the GOGI techniques is based on the belief that understandable information (referred to as DATA) must be provided within a context. This new context (referred to as SPACE) is where the individual can draw alternative conclusions and develop new cognitions, or ways of thinking.

The combination of SPACE + DATA + a perceptual SHIFT leads to new behaviors (CHANGE.) Therefore, the formula for lasting change is:

$$SPACE + DATA + SHIFT = CHANGE$$

RapidChange Therapy techniques and theories are designed to help you by:

- Creating optimal SPACE for this information to be tested and practiced.
- This SPACE affords the individual perceptual SHIFTS of thinking and awareness.
- Providing DATA in the form of understandable information.
- And, supporting the inevitable CHANGE which occurs as a result of DATA and SPACE and perceptual SHIFT availability.

In other words, GETTING OUT BY GOING IN has found that the concepts of RapidChange Therapy helps the GOGI coaches as they help others to help themselves.

**The RapidChange Therapy
Formula for Change:**

SPACE + DATA + SHIFT=CHANGE

SPACE is mental room to consider the information. DATA is information. This gives you the opportunity for perceptual SHIFT. CHANGE is the new habits which form.

GOGI is uses RapidChange Therapy to empower at-risk and incarcerated individuals to make powerful decisions.

This book is based on techniques of RapidChange Therapy (RCT), which is a unique psychological modality for rapid and lasting change. It combines traditional clinical psychology, universal human ethics and time-proven strategies for success. RCT allows for rapid change in thinking and behavior; and is this synthesis of tools for the Body, Mind and Spirit.

If asked to define RapidChange Therapy, it is helpful to call upon well-known psychological theories that are similar: Cognitive Behavioral Therapy (CBT) is similar to RapidChange Therapy. Both are based on the fact that cognitions (understanding) and behaviors are teamed to promote change. Solutions Focused Therapy is similar to RapidChange Therapy because both theories focus on the goal, or intended outcome. Brief Therapy is similar to RapidChange Therapy because it does not take a long time to get change to happen. Brief therapy does not require deep discussions of the "etiology" (a psychological term for origin) of a problem.

RapidChange Therapy is a blend of successful psychological theories and is at the core of the GOGI curriculum and intent. It presents techniques which are global in their effectiveness and is a WAY of making change happen. RapidChange Therapy supports the GOGI goals of empowering individuals to make positive decisions in their lives. It is not exclusive to the setting of incarceration. RapidChange Therapy can be used with any individual and just about any of life's challenges.

So the journey begins...

Hopefully, you will accept and welcome the intent of this material. It can empower you to realize that life can be amazing, enjoyable, beneficial, productive and peaceful, regardless of where you wake up each morning. The information lays the foundation for you to begin this portion of the journey toward internal freedom — and get out of prison before your release.

GETTING OUT BY GOING IN (GOGI) is the non-profit organization that sponsors this book. GOGI was named for the process of GETTING OUT of prison by GOING IN to the freedom only found inside of you. The material is based on volunteer work with hundreds of inmates who offered input and suggested modifications. Their insight helped form the simplicity of the tools presented.

We can all find internal freedom regardless of what kind of prison that we are in. It could be a prison of addiction, negative attitude, unproductive habits, or the inability to move beyond pain and anguish. It could be the prison of a harmful relationship, the absence of love, or the limits of a broken and disabled body.

Whatever prison confines you, there is a freedom residing within. How speedily you embrace your own internal freedom is for you to determine. The material is offered to anyone who is interested in their potential for internal freedom.

The People of GOGI

Coach DJ poses with George, David and a volunteer who contributed to the design and painting of the WALL OF SUCCESS.
The youth are graduates of the Sign Up for Success! Program for empowering youth to make positive decisions before they turn to trouble.

CHAPTER TWO
GOALS AND OUTCOMES

GETTING OUT BY GOING IN or GOGI (Pronounced Go-Gee like Yogi Bear) focuses on three areas of self-awareness and psychological development in a series of workshops, lectures, books, workbooks, group and individual discussions.

It takes an inward awareness and growth of the Body, Mind and Spirit to create the opportunity for internal freedom.

The good news for you is that internal freedom is available to all individuals. It is free of charge. It is your birthright. It is far more satisfying than any other human state of being. All it takes is unwavering dedication, singular focus and a solid commitment to change your life.

Changing your life must be a matter of life and death for you. It must be so important that no amount of suffering, struggle or obstacle can knock you off your path.

The tools presented in this book are designed to offer the opportunity for growth through expansion of skills and understanding.

The tools are designed with truth at the core; it takes growth in the three areas of Body, Mind and Spirit for lasting internal freedom to be realized.

1) **BODY** – The goal of this book is to educate participants with a basic working comprehension of the physiological process of thought and actions.

   When an individual learns why thoughts take place and how they affect the body and resulting reactions they are empowered to make stronger decisions. In a very real sense, knowledge is power.

2) **MIND** – The goal of this book is also to provide cognitive tools, or those tools that help participants build a new understanding. This will help modify perception of available options and almost always results in behavioral change.

   Understanding how the mind functions and how to empower your mind for personal freedom is an essential step in getting out of prison before your release.

3) **SPIRIT** – Finally, the goal of this book includes making the leap from existing with a fear-based, myopic, single focused or limited perspective, to a more global interpretation of options and strategies for success.

   This broadened view results in the ability to build rapport with others, increase social functioning and positively enhances the capability for lasting relationships necessary to support success.

Words from a brother...

This is going to blow you away. In order to understand my opportunities I gotta know how my body works, especially my brain. I know I have power only over me.

Whatever I think, I can do because a thought becomes and idea. An idea becomes an action. And it all depends on what action is taken, negative or positive.

The body, and my brain. So, now I am understanding the thought process. The first goal is taking getting myself together before I can help anybody else. Now I have learned to think of good things. Then I have good ideas. If I have good ideas, I can put those to action.

The mind is part of my body. The mind is powerful. The mind will play tricks on you. My mind has led my body to do things it shouldn't do because my mind was filled with wrong thoughts. My spirit was trying its best to warn me with that strong feeling but I ignored it with alcohol and drugs.

The tools that I learned with GETTING OUT BY GOING IN is to re-form my thoughts because if you re-form it means you are in control. If I am in control then I am the boss of my own brain.

Now, the spirit. This right here is deep. Because I now understand that I am a spiritual being having this experience. This is like real serious for me.

I don't know if you want to hear this or not. But I am not a religious man. I am a spiritual man. Because God is a spirit. Each time you take a breath it has the gift of God because God is a spirit. The spirit is pure and it dwells in each of us.

During this human experience the body can ignore the spirit. That is why the Mind the Body and the Spirit must work together. The reason why I learned to Get Out by Going In was I learned to get out of my body and to go into my spirit.

But again. With all three of these aspects of us, the BODY the MIND and the SPIRIT, they all must work as they were intended to be used. I freed myself before the BOP freed me. This is why I stay in good spirits. It's possible, if you want it. Only if you want it.

And it all begins with breathing. Breathing goodness and exhaled everything that is negative. People ask, "How did you do 16 years and still be in good spirits?" And I say, "the new found information and education that I have has actually helped me get out by going in. And I am staying in."

BUT CAN CHANGE TRULY LAST?

Lasting change requires commitment, support and consistent reinforcement until new neurological habits of cognition and behavior are solidified within the human physiology.

Yes, change can truly last. Change can last a lifetime. Once the desired changes take place, additional opportunities to support the new behavior must be available.

The RapidChange Therapy Equation for Change (SPACE + DATA + SHIFT = CHANGE) includes adequate support of the change in order to maintain the desired results.

WHO CAN CHANGE?

Change is possible for…
Small children, teenagers, adults, aging adults, blacks, whites, smokers, non-smokers, Christians, Muslims, Jews, Agnostics, Atheists, Romanians, Hungarians, Gypsies, overweights, underweights, addicts, AA members, bowlers, stamp collectors, readers, non-readers, Asians, Hispanics, Indians, American Indians, Canadians, Europeans, Australians, gays, lesbians, non-English speaking, English speaking, single moms, single dads, couples, families, inmates, former inmates, convicts, preachers, politicians, guards, teachers, anger issue individuals, the employed and the unemployed, the happy and the sad, and all those who may not fall into the categories mentioned above.

BUT WHAT IF IT IS TOO HARD?

If the community or family environment is not supportive of your change, or unable to help you, the burden of your change will be completely on you. You can do it, however. You **can** make it. You can review the material regularly as a consistent reinforcement of the SPACE + DATA + SHIFT = CHANGE equation.

In the setting of incarceration, graduates of the GETTING OUT BY GOING IN course are often encouraged to become "Peer Coaches" and mentor or teach others within their communities. The process of the "student" becoming the "teacher" is widely recognized as a successful support strategy and further solidifies lasting change.

If you are *serious* about making lasting changes in your life you can teach what you have learned to your cellie or son or wife or neighbor. A powerful way to support your change is to offer the teaching to your family. Tell them about the tools when you send them letters or speak with them at visits or on the telephone.

You may find they begin to appreciate your subtle commitment to creating a powerfully positive life for yourself. You may inspire them to become more successful in their own lives.

CAN I SUCCESSFULLY CHANGE?

Yes. Anyone anywhere can successfully change. There are, however, predictors of success, or elements or situations that show up as indicators of probable success.

The following "Predictors of Success," in the GOGI program are based on participant self reports and clinical observation of more than 500 incarcerated individuals.

Words from a brother...

Can change last? Hell, yeah, change can last. And it's happening on a daily basis. But the thing is, we're going to use a verb. Chang-ing. Because that means it is a continuing process. That is why I don't like to use the word change, because change is complete. I change on a daily basis. Change lasts if I practice it on a daily basis.

Somehow, the days turn into weeks and weeks turn into months and months turn into years. So its all still changing. As long as it is the change for the good, keeping your mind filled with rightness your body will follow. And your spirit strengthens. On a daily basis. So to ask me, does change last? Only if you want it to last.

Incarcerated individuals who have found internal freedom and have been successful in the process of change and are most likely to be:

1) Successful Individuals Who Enjoy a Broad Range of Experiences:

Successful individuals will apply the GOGI tools and RapidChange Therapy techniques across a broad range of experiences for full integration.

You will be more successful if you look at your entire life from the perspective of the curriculum tools. It will help to apply the tools throughout your day in all circumstances to obtain maximum benefits. If you only apply the tools in certain environments, for example at work, you are limiting your growth.

2) Successful Individuals Who Enjoy a Broad Range of Relationships:

Successful individuals apply the GOGI techniques when interacting with family members, prison staff or others during work and even on phone conversations.

Successful individuals practice new ways of listening, speaking and reacting with a wide group of people. This permits competencies in areas previously considered weak or needing work.

3) Successful Individuals Who Share Information:

Sharing the techniques and information affirms new learning. Inmates who teach or explain the process to others are far more likely to integrate the RapidChange Therapy and additional change tools into their daily lives.

Words from a brother…

Anybody can successfully change. When your Mind, your Body, and your Spirit is working together, no one can influence you to do anything you don't already want to do; not the homeboys in the yard, your girl, your family. It's all what you want to do.

I am successfully changing through the techniques and education that I've learned.

The funny thing about RapidChange Therapy is I knew it before I even knew the words. It was something I couldn't identify with words. GETTING OUT BY GOING IN didn't bring anything out of me that wasn't already there.

And that's real. It didn't make me do anything that I am not already supposed to be doing. These words I am giving you is major game. I won yesterday. I won the day before that. I been winning for the last 14 months.

And when I play the game of life tomorrow. I'm gunna protect the plate, watch for them curves and breaking balls, and make my fans (my mind, my body and my spirit) cheer for me. Those are my fans, my mind, my body and my spirit.

They say the game is to be sold not told. But I am breaking this off for free. Keep coming if you want it, because I got it. Anybody can successfully change, if they want to. Some of us become successful in the game, the drug game, or whatever game it was that was negative.

But that street life has no bearing in reality. That only belongs in the streets. It does not belong in the real world. Street life cannot blend with reality.

Step on this side of the street, play'a.

WHAT ABOUT FAMILY INVOLVEMENT?

In many cases, family involvement proves to be the most positive determining factor in the long-term success of reunification, especially among adolescents, teens, and young adults.

Having a supportive family helps all individuals. Families may not know how to or fail in adequately supporting fundamental changes when loved ones return home. Old and destructive patterns might naturally resurface and it becomes nearly impossible to sustain positive change.

This is why you must be very, very committed to new habits and not let the behaviors of others pull you off track. If your family, your job, your neighborhood, your environment cannot support you then you must support yourself fully, totally, completely.

Family members might be well-meaning but prove to be weak supporters. They might have a difficult time thinking of you in any other way than how you used to be. For as long as you have been down, they may still remember that "old" version. However, it is possible for them to see the "new" version in the long run, so do not be discouraged.

It is challenging for any human to see that someone has changed. For some reason we humans tend to feel comfortable with things that we are familiar with, even if it is not the best trait or situation.

If your family does not recognize or support the desired change, they may box you into a situation, which can steer you to return to old behavior.

Upon completion of this book and the learning of the tools herein, you are encouraged to participate in integrating the GETTING OUT BY GOING IN tools in the home environment - with willing family members.

You may decide to keep the GOGI book and other books in your library of support. Think about getting a copy of this book to your family as it can be a start for them to see the "new" you.

Sending family your letters with ideas for them to use some of the GOGI tools or other self-empowerment techniques is also a way to get them used to a new you.

Teaching anyone in the family some of the techniques is also a start at developing their support for your new learning.

Sharing your positive stories of success while you are incarcerated and making lasting changes in your life is a solid start at getting the home front to support your changes.

Long before you get home, your task is to have your family understand and accept you for the changes that you have made. Teaching your family some of the tools at your disposal may prove to be strengthening positive support for change upon your release.

WHAT IF THERE IS NO "CLASS" AND I AM JUST READING THIS BOOK ON MY OWN?

In all learning environments, materials and course experience is enhanced by the instructor's delivery. If you are reading the book on your own, you can take the role of being your own "Coach." You can play the role that GETTING OUT BY GOING IN coaches provide when facilitating any of the GOGI workshops.

Much like a coach of a sports team, the first step is for you to set firm goals and stick to your desire for internal freedom. You may set the goal not to let a situation consume your thoughts. You may set the goal to become calmer. You may set the goal of increased internal peace. Each of these qualities is on the path toward internal freedom.

Words from a brother...

To those who have children and have spent many years in prison without their children, I ask myself personally, how can I help them? How can I help them get peace and understanding?

I do have family members who are in their own prison. I only try to teach them what I've learned, and only if they ask.

When I was on the inside, I never spoke about what I'm doing because our families can be extremely negative. They only know us in a negative way. Many of us on the inside do and say "I found God. I am saved." Then they go home and act and do the exact opposite. So this growth was and is something only for me. Now if I did call and let them know "Hey, I'm doing this and that," they probably would say, "That's jailhouse talk." And I, like many others, would have resentment because no one likes rejection.

I wasn't looking to get their O.K. or their praise and it probably would have discouraged me if I did because most cats on the inside say things like this over the phone but they don't act that way on the outside and their families know it. I came home not talking about it, but BEING about it.

My homeboys. I love them, they love me. But like I said before, I can feel that they are waiting in the cut for me to go back to my old ways.

Actually, the funny thing about it is, when I read my books, they became curious. So I watch them out the corner of my eye. I set my book down, position it in a certain way, go walk the yard for an hour, come back, and someone has been reading my book.

Then, one of my homies will pull me to the side and ask questions about what I'm reading. They interested. "What kinda stuff is this?" they ask. "Why do you have peace?"

With that, I let them ask me questions. So, the support for my changing is building. Its gunna take examples. Examples and being an example.

Whatever your goal might be, keep your focus clear and your intent sound. Use the tools described in the book much like a carpenter uses his tools to build a home.

You may wish to write yourself a note you keep by your bunk.

You may wish to keep a note in your pocket as a little reminder.

You may wish to create a mantra, a meditation, a prayer or an affirmation that supports the path that you've chosen to boost your empowerment.

Words from a brother...

You don't need to be in no classroom setting in order to practice this and experience this. You only need to be willing to practice it. If it is time to read, it is time to read.

You wake up on your own. You brush your teeth on your own. You can do a lot of things on your own. You can read by yourself. Hopefully, you sleep by your self...

;) Just kidding. There is no reason to not practice this just because there is no class. What I recommend is that you put yourself in a position for success and you will succeed, just as we have put ourselves in a position for failure and we fail. So if you want this, you are going to do it, if there is a class or there isn't a class, plain and simple.

GOGI COACHES INSPIRE LASTING CHANGE

If you have the benefit of attending a GETTING OUT BY GOING IN course with a GOGI Coach or Facilitator, you might instantly recognize their unique way of working with individuals.

When you begin to think in a manner that is similar to the trained GOGI coaches, then you, too, will experience positive results in your life.

Words from a brother...

Coaches are effective in two ways; clinically and by experience. It's like that two piece combo, head and body. So that's why coaches are effective.

Coach Taylor is a Coach who is effective clinically. She has answers to questions about the body. She taught me about the effects when I am frustrated my breath gets shallow, my temperature rises, my heart races, I start sweating, my hands clench, everything raises up.

My breaths are shorter when I get upset. My mind is only thinking about FIGHTING. I never thought that it starts with breathing, but it does. When I don't breathe right I don't think right. I think only about two things: I ain't gunna run (fight or flight) so I am gunna fight.

Now, Coach DJ, is a "certified" RapidChange Therapy "Coach" and has the experience of an ex-felon who has been there, done that. Coach DJ has grown up and now has involved himself in a certain fraternity for good. Coach DJ has done everything under the sun and is spiritually changing on a daily basis.

Coach DJ works with other coaches who do not have the experience that I have in the street life. And I do not have the clinical experience that they have. This is why this one-two punch is so effective. The clinical and the experience working together. One-two combo. Wow. Who ever thought I would be doing this?

This, what I am giving you is for real. Uncut. Raw. Cats who knew me back then know me on a different level these days and they respect me. This book has been validated in experience. So this relationship of the clinical and the experience is working because we are both willing. This is why it is so effective. This is why the GOGI coaches are so effective - we bring the clinical to the experience and experience to the clinical. Yin and Yang.

As far as me as a GOGI coach, I do believe everything is good. But we all make bad decisions, bad choices, make the wrong conclusions because most of us only want to please those who we seek respect from. Now my mind is filled with rightness. My spirit is filled with goodness. That is why I am doing what I am doing now. Putting my two cents in.

If my hand does not reach you, Coach Taylor was given an opportunity to develop this program and this book. Hopefully my words and her words will reach you.

The People of GOGI

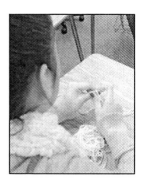

Coach DJ teaches crocheting to kids enrolled in GOGI's SIGN UP FOR SUCCESS! program in Inglewood, California. Kids learn quickly. It helps them learn focus, goal setting, and to relax.

WHAT IS THE PURPOSE OF THIS BOOK?

From the very first GETTING OUT BY GOING IN class held at Federal Prison in California, it has been the goal of GOGI to empower individuals to make decisions, which bring internal joy, peace and happiness.

The techniques and concepts in this book have helped people with bad tempers to rapidly deal with their temper. The techniques have helped people to overcome feeling ashamed of their life or situation and begin to teach others powerful techniques of internal freedom. And the techniques and concepts have helped people who are locked away from their children, become involved in their children's lives.

This book is designed to provide tools to help you make your life wonderful - right now, today, and at this very moment. It is likely that your experience of integrating and diligently living the concepts of these simple tools will result in a successful, lasting re-entry into society.

Words from a brother...
Will it work for you? Hell, yeah it will work for you. But you can't go in half stepping. Ya feel me?
All or nothing. Make sure in the beginning that you are around people on the same frequency that you are on, and it will work.

But more importantly than lasting reentry is the internal freedom available to you right this very minute, this very day. Optimally, your life will be a force for good. You can become one of those increasingly frequent individuals who are helping redirect the impending train wreck of society by setting a powerful example for a positive and simple life.

When you become truly successful at this thing called Life, your internal freedom will be profound, and your environment will benefit from your gentle walk on the earth. When you are successful at this thing called Life, your positive influence will be felt anywhere you find yourself.

Words from a brother...

I met Bo Lozoff when I was at a Federal Prison and he came to do a workshop. He was sitting on top on a table playing guitar and talking to us. He was sitting in the easy pose.

I explained to him that once I had the understanding of how to get in tune with inner peace the vibration (I call them radio signals) to get in tune with inner peace and send those radio signals out I would start thinking different, feeling different, acting different. He was tripping.

We spoke about some things like intention and he said," I see that you have been making breakthroughs. Now, I am attracting different people. It is a good feeling that I have.

I glanced through his book and I see that he has been giving with his Human Kindness Foundations. Giving people what he has. And with those signals, they will be received by people on the same frequency.

Once I have done that, again, on a daily basis, I unlocked that spiritual door that I had blocked for many years. I unblocked the mental blocks. And on May 8th, 2-0-0-6, my body was freed from being locked up since Feb. 6, 1990. Now like my friend says, I am living the life my soul has intended for me to live. The purpose of this book is to do just that. Free your mind and the rest will follow.

Your intentions are everything. It is the Alpha. The beginning. No hidden agendas. If you are open, willing and honest, I guarantee you will be successful. Let's tune into the same station...KGOGI = lasting freedom.

If you want what was given to me you can cop this book.

HOW DOES INTERNAL FREEDOM HAPPEN?

The first set of tools presented in the tools section - Section One, (BODY), provides a foundation for understanding and learning.

Parts of the brain are explored and placed into simple concepts. If you know what is under the hood of a car it usually makes you a more informed car owner or driver.

Similarly, if you know how and why your brain works, you are likely to be more successful in your quest for internal freedom.

The second set of tools is presented in Section Two, (MIND), and provides cognitive tools to bring about change in current behavior so that immediate improvement may be experienced. In this section, additional simple tools are provided which enable you to get in the driver's seat of your life.

Section Three, (SPIRIT), provides the opportunity to support expanding knowledge and to provide a roadmap to be referred to throughout life's experiences.

Seeing beyond the immediate or the obvious is a powerful tool for internal freedom.

The linear progression of learning presented in the GETTING OUT BY GOING IN materials provides you with optimal results when you apply each tool in a focused manner for an entire week before moving on to the next.

The tools described in this book are most effective if practiced over a six-week period with a "completion" or "graduation" celebration for your progress at the end of the work.

Words from a brother...

All internal happiness just happens naturally when we are ready and willing. It's like becoming a cup. A cup is always ready to receive what is put inside of it. So become a cup. But you have to watch what you pour inside that cup, positive or negative.

Once you know that there is positive-ness inside the body, you begin the process. That is the starting point, putting positive-ness inside the cup.

Life is whatever you are making it to be. It has to be the correct ingredients. It doesn't mean changing certain parts of you, it means changing everything about you.

Change stays happening naturally, if you are willing to let it work for you.

YEAH, BUT WILL IT WORK FOR ME?

The measure of your success from this material is proportional to the amount of effort that you put into it.

Those individuals who go to the gym and pump a little iron every day eventually begin to wear their results. Those individuals who put away a couple dollars a day are eventually able to buy a home, car, or a vacation.

Those individuals who meditate each day will eventually accumulate a wealth of relaxation that sets them apart from their friends.

Those individuals who learn and apply the concepts described in this book also reap the rewards of their efforts over time, and in subtle increments.

The tools learned each week will undoubtedly improve your life by helping you to make positive choices. When presented and incorporated into daily life, you will gain further understanding of how those choices are made.

Will this book work for you?

This book WILL work for you – if you are ready to do the work. Again, the measure of your success is entirely proportional to the amount of effort you put into it.

Those individuals who pick up a book for a few minutes each day will eventually accumulate a wealth of knowledge that sets them apart from their friends.

The People of GOGI

Coach Felicia talks about GOGI to a prospective volunteer.

GOGI Coach / Facilitators acknowledge the following positive attributes in everyone:

GOGI Coaches Believe...

➢ People are more good than bad.

➢ "Negative" or "bad" behavior usually stems from poor coping tools, limited support, or misinformation.

➢ People innately want to be good, successful and to positively contribute to life and the ones they love.

➢ People sometimes lack the knowledge or support to be good, successful, or positively contribute to life.

➢ Some people get frustrated and act out when they do not get the help they need. Many individuals do not know how to ask for the help they need.

➢ People may behave poorly out of bad habits, and/or they may be frightened, disappointed, insecure, scared, angry, or do not know other ways of being.

➢ Peers are more influential teachers of behavior than academic teachers. Behaviors are more easily changed with peer group support.

➢ People develop new, more productive, habits that become automatic with practice.

➢ People respond well to positive reinforcement.

➢ People's weak areas improve with an awareness of and a focus on their strengths.

➢ People's strengths can be utilized as tools for change.

➢ People's lives get better when honesty, trustworthiness, integrity, and honor are incorporated into their behavior.

TOOLS FOR THE BODY

CHAPTER THREE
LET GO... FORGIVE...
& CLAIM RESPONSIBILITY

YOUR EARLY RELEASE

Many individuals believe that they are trapped or imprisoned — even if they are not in a physical prison run by a State, or the BOP. Getting out of the prison of limited or faulty thinking can be a bigger challenge than a physical prison because it means letting go, forgiving and claiming responsibility for your life. This causes discomfort. But keep going.

By making use of the tools in this book, you may begin to see signs of an early release from a self-imposed solitary confinement. The signs, however, may be subtle.

You may notice a new calmness in your daily life. It may be that someone comments, "What's up with you?" or "What's going on?" or "Are you doing OK?"

It is likely that you will feel more relaxed, can sleep better, and smile a bit more.

Friends or family may not understand this as positive change, and they may voice concern, criticism or even contempt. As you communicate in new ways, you are sending new messages through new actions or by non-actions. This may disturb the comfort level of those closest to you.

If you continue on your path, you might perhaps find new and different opportunities to learn and grow, and notice individuals and places in ways that are surprisingly refreshing.

It is likely, also, that you will have a wider perception of your own possibilities. If this is the case, then it is the time to set some goals for yourself, both personally and professionally.

You are in a powerful position for change and transformation with new tools like those that are described in this book.

DATA must be presented within enough SPACE and perceptual SHIFT for lasting CHANGE to occur.

DATA (information) is presented in the materials of this book. Give yourself the time (SPACE) to let change occur through perceptual widening, or a greater understanding leading to CHANGE.

Stay consistent with the SPACE + DATA + SHIFT = CHANGE equation and you will truly experience personal mastery.

Remember, you will need to sustain that CHANGE long enough to have the change solidify in your body's neurology, the internal wiring of your body, long enough to become a habit.

The most critical part of CHANGE is sustaining it long enough so that you do not have to repeat the same process - over and over - again.

What, then, is Internal Freedom?

Words from a brother…

This is the part I like right here. Getting out of prison spiritually first is how I freed myself. May 8th is when the BOP freed me. These tools would mean nothin, if I DIDN'T APPLY THEM WHEN THE bop freed me. I am doing volunteer work and teaching kids what I have learned from GOGI. I am being a better person today. I am being a better brother, better friend. In my human experience before, I wasn't a nice guy. Now that I am free, mind body and soul, I am a good human being today. And I am going to do it again tomorrow. I will always remember the pain of 16 years, 3 months, two days. That is why I am sharing it with you right now. Always remember that. It's not about just getting out of prison. Or, what you are going to do to stay out of prison. It is what you are going to do on a daily basis. I told my friend that, "Yes, I have done all that time but my spirit does not feel that I ever went there." No more commissary. No more bunk beds. No more 4 o'clock counts. No more 10 minute movements. I haven't thought about that until right now. I thought I was getting soft but I am getting stronger. Because I am working at it. I get paid $9.00 an hour at an auto shop. Crazy, huh? I used to push them bricks and hold them pistols. Now I am pushing as a street sweeper and holding a Windex bottle. All I'm doing is squeezing a trigger and shooting Windex. Dramatic change, huh? But it's OK. It pays the bills. But this is just the beginning. I'm not too big to do this. It's very humbling. Hmmm.

FACT: INTERNAL FREEDOM COSTS

First, let's be brutally honest about Internal Freedom. Internal Freedom has a big price. No internal comes without the price being paid. It will cost you your ego and your will, two things individuals have a tendency to defend to the death.

If you are willing to pay the price of taking that lonesome and sometimes painful walk beyond the confines of your ego and bad habits, you will find that freedom is waiting.

Words from a brother...

Internal freedom costs only the willingness and practice. Nothing more. But the payoff is priceless. Because you will learn that only you control you.

If you want to experience internal freedom, you will need to pay the price in three areas of your life.

1. **LET GO.** You will need to let go. This means you need to let go of resentments, pain inflicted to or from another, heartaches, and grudges.

2. **FORGIVE.** You will need to forgive yourself and all others. Close the door on the pain of the past as you focus on your internal freedom from the influences of others.

3. **RESPONSIBILITY.** You will need to assume total responsibility in your life.

Let's look at each area to see if you can identify clear ways to get yourself closer to total and complete responsibility for your thoughts and actions and subsequently, the results that you produce in your life.

LET GO

Letting go is very difficult when you are not certain how far you are going to fall.

Fear is the greatest obstacle to change. We fear what we do not know. What we fear we do not embrace. So, we repeat our failures over and over again because we are fearful of what will happen to us if we change.

Individuals often remain in destructive relationships, unfulfilling occupations, and unhealthy bodies and minds due to fear of the unknown. They do not clearly see what it would be like to experience things differently.

It is easier for governments and large organizations to manipulate the masses because people generally do not want to "let go" of current ways of thinking and limit the exploration or desire to try out new ways. They complain. They blame. But they rarely let go.

Most individuals do not want to let go of their sense of "security" no matter how detrimental it is to their own life. Individuals habitually "grab on" to more and more and more.

Consequently, we have huge homes, huge cars, huge storage units, huge debt, huge anxiety, huge depression and huge lack of time. How can you swim against the prevailing tide and begin to do things differently?

Inside the "laboratory" or the institution of "Higher Learning" represented by the four walls holding you in place, you have the opportunity to develop and flex the muscle of personal mastery of internal freedom.

FLEX YOUR MUSCLES

Your stay in prison is intended to be a punishment but it is possible to use your time as a rare opportunity for your personal empowerment.

Your incarceration can be experienced from many different perspectives. Your ability to flourish and thrive behind bars is entirely dependent upon the parts of your incarceration that you choose to focus on.

When forced to let things go, you have the opportunity to work through the ugliness that inevitably surfaces. Then you will find the place where you are ultimately free — regardless of the walls that confine you.

YOUR RARE OPPORTUNITY BEHIND BARS

We do often not like what we see in the mirror when we are absent of all the trimmings that come with living.

Cutting off the cuffs and freeing yourself of "stuff" is the first step in letting go.

It is a rare opportunity that an individual has the opportunity to actually LET GO and start to remake their lives from a new way of looking at living.

More often than not, this process is one that individuals may not experience until they are on their deathbed. That is when individuals almost always become concerned about how they treated other individuals.

When forced with the reality of their mortality, they suddenly realize all their stuff is staying behind and the only things they take with them are the knowledge, experience, and the love expressed along the way.

What would it take for you to truly LET GO of your attachment to "stuff"?

What will it take for you to be more concerned about bringing a smile to someone instead of getting back at them for what they said, jockeying in line for food, or the filing a complaint because your boss unfairly accused you of not doing your job?

What will it take?

What will it take for you to tell your loved ones that you are willing to LET GO of anger and begin the long journey to internal freedom, and that you need their help and support throughout the process?

What will it take for you to look beyond your own myopic experience of the world around you?

Maybe you can begin to offer help others or volunteer to assist those organizations who are helping others.

Maybe you can simply help by listening more than you speak.

You can LET GO simply by taking two steps beyond the resentments, two steps beyond pain inflicted to and by another, two steps beyond the heartache and two steps beyond your grudges.

Here is what you are likely to experience if you study and master LET GO and the other techniques described in this book.

Let Go of...

- Thinking you need an expensive car.

- Thinking you need fast money.

- Thinking you need expensive clothes.

- Thinking you need a big home.

- Thinking you need a flashy girl/guy.

- Thinking you need any THING except INTERNAL FREEDOM.

- Thinking that THINGS make you more successful, powerful, desirable.

- Thinking THINGS represent freedom.

Thinking things matter at all is thinking that is a guarantee that you will not experience internal freedom. THINGS get in the way of internal freedom. THINGS are the prison. Truly let go of THINGS and....

Truly Let Go and...

- You will smile more.

- You will breathe more fully.

- You will attract truly successful individuals.

- You will earn REAL respect.

- You will see possibilities and joy where you previously experienced darkness and despair.

- You will think more people as likable or you may even find them fascinating.

- You will begin to experience the finest "drug" of all....Internal Freedom.

YOUR CHALLENGE - 60 MINUTES

Give yourself a challenge. Set aside one hour a day, just sixty short minutes.

In those sixty short minutes, make the conscious choice to use the techniques learned in this book to help you LET GO.

Maybe it is the first hour of your day when you set you mind to focus on being the best you can be.

LET GO of all those things keeping you from being your best. LET GO of thoughts regarding the U. S. President and the BOP. LET GO of thoughts of your incarceration. LET GO of thoughts about your appeal. LET GO of thoughts about your remaining years behind bars. Let GO of your accusers.

LET GO of everything that deters you from experiencing this day, this 60 minutes, as the best possible.

Start each day with MENTAL FREEDOM, having LET GO of the psychological chains that bind you to internal incarceration.

You may choose to say, "I will make today internally peaceful, regardless of my environment, LETTING GO of anything that stands in my way of internal freedom."

The truth is…the only one standing in the way of your internal freedom is YOU! Get out of your way!

In addition to LET GO, there are other steps, none more or less challenging than the others, on your journey to Getting Out of Prison Before Your Release.

NEXT…

The second step along this journey of Getting Out of Prison Before Your Release is one of FORGIVENESS OF SELF AND OTHERS.

FORGIVENESS...
OF SELF AND OTHERS

When we hold on to events of the past, we limit our potential for positive experiences. It goes back to the concept of holding-on to extra "baggage" that we no longer need.

Some people may believe that if they LET GO they will be subjected to the same type of pain, and the same experience all over again.

We, as humans, automatically store our experiences in subconscious memory, just in case we need to remember or protect ourselves from similar ones.

The brain is wonderfully efficient and logs our suffering. We remember the suffering and attempt to avoid it, but inevitably recreate it time and time again because we have a fixed focus on the suffering.

It is almost as if by NOT forgiving — we doom ourselves to remain in the cycle of recreating the very thing we wish to avoid.

If you have a friend and he steals from you, then it is not wise to leave your wallet out in the open. That's just not smart. It is not protecting you and it may be tempting him beyond his ability to resist.

What forgiveness means is that you protect yourself through a positive and proactive perspective, not from a negative or reactionary approach. It also means that you don't leave your wallet out to tempt anyone. Consider your surroundings. You have control over where you leave your wallet.

Clearly defined boundaries

Forgiveness of yourself means that you protect yourself enough so that you do not invite experiences that require forgiveness.

Stay away from troublemakers or those whose integrity or honor is questionable. Stay true to your word and expect that others will do the same.

With established boundaries that are clearly and calmly stated, you are raising the bar of the behavior of those around you.

Having clearly defined boundaries means that you will need to forgive less often because individuals will behave differently around you.

Walking beyond your past

FORGIVENESS means walking beyond past negative experiences and strengthening yourself internally so that you are aware and prepared to avoid such experiences in the future.

FORGIVENESS requires you to LET GO.

To LET GO and the art of FORGIVENESS of self and others work harmoniously with each other.

CONSIDER THIS...

Tonight as the lights go out and you are left with your thoughts, consider what it would be like to live completely free of memories that might require your forgiveness.

What would you feel like if you had nothing or no one to forgive? How would you sleep if there were nothing in your life to forgive? What would your day be like tomorrow if you had nothing more to forgive?

If you are willing to be free, truly free, you will let go and forgive. As you drift off to sleep, let your subconscious mind muse at the possibility of releasing ill feelings toward yourself and others.

In releasing these thoughts and feelings, you are empowered to move beyond the confines, the "prison," of holding on.

ASSUME TOTAL RESPONSIBILITY

The final step toward Getting Out of Prison Before Your Release is to accept total responsibly for your life. Total responsibly permits you to claim ownership of your life. Total responsibility puts you in control of the events of your life.

Someone may ask, "Are you saying I caused my father to beat me?" or "You mean I am responsible for the poverty I was born into?"

It would surely be extremely naive, even disrespectful to claim that another individual is the cause of misfortune or abuse that comes your way. This is not the case.

If your father beat you, or you were born into poverty, however, it does not give you the right or the excuse to be anything less than a wonderful and peaceful human being.

Your REACTIONS define you

There are countless autobiographies and biographies of individuals of every culture, race, creed, color religion and who raise themselves from "rags to riches", moving beyond the confines of their childhood into powerful positions within their communities.

Believe it or not, your life, regardless of the darkness of its history, may be molded and shaped by you to reflect a "rags to riches" scenario of internal accomplishments. Your "dark" history can be the key to your bright future.

It is not easy to be a REAL success. It takes determination and dedication. It takes an unwavering dedication. It takes letting go of every THING that gets in the way of your freedom. Let it go. It is not worth it. Easy money is not worth it.

Easy money is cheap, lazy, false, fake, and disappears as soon as the Feds break down the door and yell "FREEZE!" Go for the REAL gold, the gold that comes from INTERNAL FREEDOM. Let THAT shine.

You are responsible

The fact is: you are totally RESPONSIBLE for your REACTIONS. Your REACTIONS to things, events, places and people are your RESPONSIBILITY.

And in a very real way, your reactions create your reality. Your perceptions affect your level of responsibility and your reactions. How you think about an event determines your reaction.

What happens to your physical body may be up to God, Allah, Buddha, Fate, Karma or bad luck of the draw. How you REACT to what happens is totally and completely YOUR RESPONSIBILITY.

When you ASSUME TOTAL RESPONSIBILITY, you move into the most powerful position that any individual can experience.

You become a creator of your experience. Pick and choose those things that you endorse as desirable and steer clear of those things that do not serve you.

Stop blaming others...

Countless inmates blame the system, staff, warden, buddies, wives, co-defendants, witnesses, DA, the government, or environment for their internal condition.

Every time you blame someone else for anything, you are recreating negative thoughts within your mind.

You are feeding your mind with negative thoughts when you say, "If the warden were not such a...." or "If she would only..." or "If I were not locked up, then I would not be depressed..." or "How can I not be angry, you have no idea what I am going through!"

Negative thoughts keep you stuck in the web of "their" control. Get out of their web. Walk away from the negative thoughts.

There are changes that occur in an inmate when they finally LET GO, FORGIVE and ASSUME TOTAL RESPONSIBILITY.

Their faces brighten. A smile replaces a frown. Posture straightens and they select words differently. Good things begin to happen to them. Somehow, the world seems to be a better place when these people are nearby.

GETTING OUT OF PRISON BEFORE YOUR RELEASE

Getting Out of Prison Before Your Release comes at a cost. Countless individuals have paid that price. And as difficult as it is, as frightening as the journey may be, as daunting of a task as it appears, no one regrets their decision to:

- LET GO
- FORGIVE
- CLAIM RESPONSIBILITY

The path to INTERNAL FREEDOM and GETTING OUT OF PRISON BEFORE YOUR RELEASE will take you through Letting Go, Forgiveness and Assuming Total Responsibility for Your Life.

Remember: 30 percent of inmates never ever come back to prison. That is a lot of individuals who decide to change their lives. You can be one of those people.

You can help raise the statistic to 31 percent. Teach your cellie and you can help make it 32 percent. With enough inmates learning to LET GO, FORGIVE and CLAIM RESPONSIBILITY the INMATES can make prisons obsolete.

Traditional religions, ancient spiritual cultures and spiritual practices such as yoga and meditation attempt to nudge you in the direction of internal peace.

The concepts of LET GO, FORGIVE and TOTAL RESPONSIBILITY are a part of these practices, as well as being universal.

Tools of internal freedom are taught in many different forms with many different names.

The GOGI approach and the techniques herein attempt to provide you with enough DATA to create enough internal SPACE to support SHIFT and the inevitable CHANGE that occurs.

> *We either live a life where we choose how we react to situations or we abdicate our power and let life live us, permitting others and situations to determine our destiny.*
>
> *Prison is letting situations drive you to actions which do not help you live a clean, drug free, crime free, depression free, and anger free life.*
>
> *At every moment of every day we are either living our life or we are letting our life live us.*
>
> *Coach Taylor*

You can contribute positively to those around you

As you speak openly, and without judgment of others, you might inspire others when you share your own internal journey.

Strength comes from sharing — we never really learn a concept until we are able to teach it to someone else.

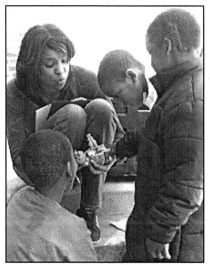

Coach ReNina teaches the GOGI concepts to kids in Watts, California.

Volunteers Dave Reichard and Tom Melgun take a short break in the GOGI Offices.

GOGI Coach DJ with his mother, Cathy. This picture was taken at a restaurant. It was the first time in 16 years Cathy celebrated her birthday in a restaurant instead of a prison visiting room.

CHAPTER FOUR
BOSS OF YOUR BRAIN

The first "tool" you have in the journey to internal freedom is knowledge; knowledge about your physical body.

When you gain knowledge about any subject you have the ability to improve and direct ideas, thoughts and actions related to the new knowledge.

When someone learns about the parts of the car under the hood, they become a more informed driver. An informed driver has the opportunity to become a better driver.

In this chapter, you will be given permission to look under the hood of your car, so to speak. You will learn just a little bit about how your brain functions.

Through this knowledge, you will have the opportunity to become BOSS OF YOUR BRAIN.

For best results in making change happen, read this chapter every night for a full week. Focus on and practice the concept presented. If you skip a few days - make them up and repeat the reading again and again and again.

Sometimes making notes in the margins of the book will help you reflect on your thoughts. Oftentimes reading your notes again and again will permit you to track your own internal progress.

CREATE YOUR OWN COLLEGE

College students are taught the value of making notes about their studies in notebooks or in the margins of their books. In truth, they are no smarter than you. They just learned that taking notes is helpful. Someone took the time to teach them how to take notes. Well, now you have no more excuses. You now have learned that note taking empowers you.

What you do with it is up to you. Don't worry about spelling. The notes are for your eyes only. It is your book. Mark it up as much as you want. The fact is that taking notes empowers you to learn more. Be like a successful college student and take notes or ignore the advice.

Read any book over and over again and you will learn new things from reflecting on your notes in the margins. Now that you know that taking notes can be helpful, you can put into practice something that has helped college students for centuries.

Make notes about what you read, reflect on your learning and incorporate what you read into your daily thoughts. Move to the next chapter only when you are confident that you have integrated and added the previous learning to your toolbox of change.

Also, give yourself time for the process of change to unfold. If this book sits by your bed for a couple of months, just open one page and read it moments before lights out. Glance over your notes, and reflect on the process of change.

Thirty seconds of nightly reflection, when added over the weeks and months, brings immeasurable results. Even if it is only thirty seconds of reading — having positive and helpful information nearby can offer great support.

Most importantly, remember that change takes time. Please do yourself a favor and let the process of change unfold naturally. Make time to practice each tool so you may experience the positive changes that others found possible with these simple tools.

LET'S GET STARTED

Many individuals believe that their brain is not controllable; and, that their brain controls them. "It's just the way I am," often becomes the automatic response when life gets out of control. This is simply not true.

Your brain operates much like a car. You can drive it wherever you want to, but if you take your hands off the wheel, the car might spin out of control or go in another direction. Your brain is yours to change, mold and shape to do exactly what you want it to do. Simply put, you (and only you) are the **BOSS OF YOUR BRAIN.**

Difficulty in controlling your actions or thoughts stems from not understanding your personal abilities and powers, and from neglecting your right to create desired thoughts or behavior.

As you learn how the brain functions, you are likely to make an effort to control your thoughts rather than to buy into the concept of "It's just the way I am."

Learning the basics about how your brain functions is like learning to drive. For example, consider when a 16-year-old "gets" to know how a car works. By learning to operate the vehicle with increasing skill and efficiency, he/she is able to keep the vehicle on the road and inside the designated lanes.

Compare how you control, alter, modify and change your brain to when you are behind the wheel of a car. It may not always seem like it, but you truly have control of the vehicle called your body and your brain.

Your brain is yours to command, to direct, to steer in the direction that you, and only you, dictate. You are in the driver's seat. No one else is driving your car. You are behind the wheel — not the warden, not the guard, not your cell mate. You are the only one in control of your reactions, your thoughts and your words. Therefore, only you control your future. You and only you are the BOSS OF YOUR BRAIN.

COMFORT

Individuals often find a comfort zone within their bad habits. This comfort zone leads them to believe that their reactions and thoughts are beyond their control.

More frequently than not, incarcerated individuals have a lengthy list of habits that have perpetuated the same unproductive behavior over and over.

It is likely that recidivism rates would drop significantly if individuals understood and practiced being in control of their brain.

How can a 16-year-old drive across the country if no one told them what is under the hood of the car, or how to read a road map? It is almost impossible to drive very far without a map, or "DATA."

Although the internal nitro-fueled mental "engine" of yours might be under-nourished and under-utilized at the moment, you can be the **BOSS OF YOUR BRAIN.** You can begin making modifications right now. Today.

The **BOSS OF YOUR BRAIN** awareness will help you:

1. Take control of the way your brain processes **information**.

2. Take control of the way your brain processes **emotions**.

3. Take control of the way your brain processes **beliefs**.

THE TRUTH IS. . .

Being the
BOSS OF YOUR BRAIN
will allow you to make choices
that are entirely yours;
not society's choices,
not your situation's choices
not your parents' choices.

Being the
BOSS OF YOUR BRAIN
will allow you to make
solid decisions based
on more information,
wider perception,
and less reaction.

HOW DOES <u>BOSS OF YOUR BRAIN</u> WORK?

Let's break it down in its most simple form. You have three parts of your brain you need to know. The front part, behind your forehead, is your LOGICAL/SMART THINKING. It's actually called the EXECUTIVE FUNCTIONING area by people who study the brain. For us, we are going to call it the SMART THINKING area. SMART THINKING is at the front of the head, just behind the forehead.

The second part that you need to know is in the very center of the brain called the LIMBIC SYSTEM where emotions are processed and assigned to thoughts. We are going to call this the EMOTIONAL CONTROL CENTER. This is where we make judgments and attach feelings to things that happen.

The third area of the brain you need to know to be the BOSS OF YOUR BRAIN is the back part of your brain that we will call AUTOMATIC THINKING. In this back part of your brain you store both good and bad habits.

Knowledge of these three parts of the brain empowers you to be the BOSS OF YOUR BRAIN.

1) SMART THINKING – right behind the forehead.

2) EMOTIONAL CONTROL CENTER – in the very center of the brain.

3) AUTOMATIC THINKING – in the back of the brain where habits are stored.

WHY THE BOSS OF YOUR BRAIN WORKS

Would you start a car, put your foot on the gas, take your hands off the steering wheel, and let the car go wherever it wanted? Certainly not. But this is what you do when you do not claim your right to be the **BOSS OF YOUR BRAIN.**

Being the **BOSS OF YOUR BRAIN** works because when you know if you are focusing on SMART THINKING, AUTOMATIC THINKING or EMOTIONAL THINKING you are empowered to be the BOSS OF YOUR BRAIN. When you know the parts of your brain that respond a certain way, you will not permit the actions of a corrections officer to control you.

You will not take your hands off the steering wheel of your life and let your car run over a cliff when a guard acts inappropriately or when your cellie gets on your nerves.

Being the BOSS OF YOUR BRAIN allows you to drive your own car. Don't let someone else get behind the wheel and start controlling your ideas, thoughts or actions. Knowing what part of your brain is working enables you to remain in control.

NEURONS AND NEURO-TRANSMITTERS

Much like the electrical wiring in a house or a stereo, your body has a communication network that moves energy, or messages, from one cell of your body to the other.

In a house, a current of energy is sent from the electric pole, to the house, then to the plug or the light switch.

In the human body, information is sent from one end of the neurological communication network (the center of the brain, for example) to the other. Your mouth responds with words, your hands respond in action, and your feet respond in movement, etc. Much like tracing the fuel line of a car or the wiring of a home, your body's "wiring" can be traced.

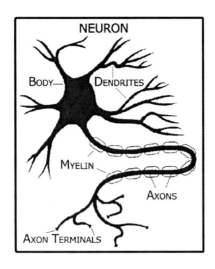

Here are the parts of your body's communication network.

- **Neuron** - A neuron is a message holder inside your body. It is a squiggly thing that kind of looks like an octopus with tentacles – called "dendrites" – at the ends.

  There are billions of these octopus-like neurons in every area of your body just waiting to deliver messages to neighboring neurons all lined up anxious to receive messages telling them what you want them to do.

  One neuron sends its message to another neuron ready to receive the message. Much like a river, the message flows through your body from one neuron to the next.

  These neurons form a web of communication, much like a spider web of connections, with messages being transmitted from a long line of dendrite endings to other dendrite endings across what is called the synaptic cleft.

- **Neurotransmitters** - Neurotransmitters are the delivery service that takes the message from one neuron to the next. Scientists called them the "neurotransmitters—since they are "transmitters" of neural messages.

  Neurotransmitters are kind of like cars on a freeway. The individual inside the car is the neuron. The car is like the neurotransmitter.

  Another analogy might be to compare neurons and neurotransmitters to floating down a river on an inner tube. The Neurotransmitter would be the water flowing down the river. The guy and the inner tube would be the message floating down the worn pathway.

  There are many types of neurotransmitters just like there are many different types of oil for automobiles and many different kinds of automobiles, trains or planes to move people around.

Here are some examples of Neurotransmitters and what they do:

ACETYLCHOLINE Most abundant in the brain Memory and thought In hippocampus Imbalance = Poor ability to concentrate; Alzheimer's
DOPAMINE Controls physical movement, attention, reward system Decreases with age Improves mood, sex drive, memory Imbalance related to Parkinson's Disease Excess: Schizophrenia
NOREPINEPHRINE Excitatory: causes the brain to be alert Vital for short-term storage into long-term Regulates sex drive, Improves mood Shortage: Depression Excess: Anxiety
SEROTONIN The "Feel Good" Transmitter Aids in smooth muscle movement Aids in smooth information transmission Shortage = Low self-esteem, depression Excess: Perfection is manorexia, violence

> *Words from a brother...*
>   *What I have learned about dopamine is that it is a pleasure chemical in the brain. Never knew that before. Now I know I don't have go buy pleasure from stores, get it from women or anything materialistic. I get pleasure out of just being alive and letting my brain know I control it. And with that, I let God run the show.*

- **Neurological Pathways** - Neurological pathways are like rivers or roads running throughout your body. Some rivers and roads are traveled over and over again. Some rivers dry up from lack of use. And some rivers form a Grand Canyon-like valley within your body because the water flows continuously and flows over the same area for years and years and years.

  A neurological pathway is a sequence of neurons that sends messages to the same neurons over and over again, much like a river sending water down the same path, over and over again.

  This pattern is repeated so much that it becomes a well-worn path through the human mind and body. It is a regular pathway of communication, a habit that you do automatically.

Your Body's Rivers of Communication

Your body has old, worn and unproductive neurological pathways that you use when you let your brain be the boss of you. They are like worn rivers and show up as habits and behaviors that you think you have no control over.

However, when you decide that you are the BOSS OF YOUR BRAIN your body can create new, powerful and productive neurological pathways regardless of your age, size, shape, color, religion, sex, or intelligence.

The fact is that you can build new neurological pathways any time you wish, at any age. Instead of letting the AUTOMATIC THINKING part of your brain take you into old habits, you can – I promise you – you CAN build new and improved habits if you use the front part of your brain, your SMART THINKING.

Every individual can make new neurological pathways. When you let your mind boss itself, the neurons and neurotransmitters repeat old thoughts, old behaviors, and old ways of being and you feel as if you have no control over your actions or thoughts. You are AUTOMATIC THINKING, replaying old habits stored in the back of your brain.

However even though bad habits allow your <u>body</u> to be the boss—you can take over any time that you like. You and only you can become the Boss of Your Brain.

When you are the BOSS OF YOUR BRAIN, then you choose where the neurons send their messages.

HOW TO BE THE BOSS OF YOUR BRAIN

STEP 1) INFORMATION IN - This process is physiologically complex, but to keep it simple let's assume that all information comes into the very center of your brain for processing through your sense of sight, smell, touch, hearing and taste. It comes in and finds its way to the EMOTIONAL CONTROL CENTER. This is where it is assigned meaning, a judgment is made.

STEP 2) ELECTRICAL CURRENT - Much like an electrical current taking power from a light switch to a bulb, this information shoots through your body with a meaning attached. You decide what things are, and what they mean based on previous experiences and goals.

STEP 3) AUTOMATIC THINKING – When your old habits begin to AUTOMATICALLY take over, you need to get the thought back to the SMART THINKING AREA, in the front of your brain.

STEP 4) INSERT A WEDGE - You can cut the current of old meaning, actually re-route the neurons by sending thoughts to your SMART THINKING area, the front of your brain. Getting the thought up to the front creates a neurological WEDGE. This "wedge" or the rerouting of information could possibly buy you just enough time to avoid many of the automatic mistakes. Your mistakes are likely to be old neurological habits that are tucked in the back of your brain.

WEDGE?

Breathing can be considered a wedge. Walking the yard may be a wedge. Going to speak to a Chaplain may be a wedge. Meditating may be a wedge. Lifting weights may be a wedge. Dominoes may be a wedge. Reading may be a wedge. Whatever you do, take the thought out of the AUTOMATIC THINKING part of your brain and get it up front, behind your forehead, to your SMART THINKING area.

STEP 5) 21 DAYS – ADDICTIONS BE GONE - A majority of the prisoners behind bars in America are more addicts than they are criminals. They are addicts who commit crimes. What would happen if every prison taught prisoners how to break addictions by using BOSS OF YOUR BRAIN as a tool? What would happen if you broke YOUR addictions by taking your addictive thoughts out of the AUTOMATIC THINKING area for 21 days and you really focused on SMART THINKING for 21 days?

Do you realize that if you drink a glass of water rather than light up a cigarette for 21 days, it is likely that you will have a new habit of drinking water instead of rushing to a cigarette? It's true. Try it.

If you build and support a new neurological habit long enough then meth, coke, chronic, cigarettes, or cell-made wine has no power over you.... none at all. You rewire your brain to NOT INCLUDE the neurology of the old habit.

When you get a new job it usually takes about 21 days before the tasks become automatic and do not take a lot of thought. Tasks move from the front part of your brain, SMART THINKING, to the AUTOMATIC THINKING part of your brain. Work becomes easier.

It takes about 21 days for your body's neurology to build a habit. The exciting fact is that **you may start to rewire your body's habits today.** This can vary depending on your body's unique operating system and the subject of the new information

It takes about 21 days for your body to replace an old habit and make a new neurological habit. Run your new neurological habit for 21 days and it will become your new neurological river. Stay away from old traps, fortify the new neurology, and stay in SMART THINKING.

Scary Santa

Many kids cry the first time they experience a smiling, heavy-set, bearded man in a bright red suit asking them to sit on his lap and tell him their inner most desires. Santa can be pretty scary the first time around.

A child naturally responds to the limited information available to them. Until additional information is provided, they are running on instinct. Once they are trained that the fat man in the red suit means gifts, the experience is less frightening and they look forward to December 25th.

Santa, and everything else, is assigned meaning based on our experiences and interpretation. Until we see the presents, we are not really anxious to sit on the fat man's lap and have our picture taken.

The bad news is that we often times assume that society's traditional and automatic assumptions, our family's assumptions and the assumptions we develop from our past experience are correct. The good news is that we can re-route our assumptions to new neurological pathways at any time in our lives

The Assigned Meaning

Along with my team of coaches, I volunteer at an elementary school in Watts, California. I teach the children GOGI techniques to help them make stronger life choices in the future. One of the first days that I was on the playground with the kids, I heard what I thought was a car backfiring.

> *"Let's go over there," one of the fifth grade boys suggested as he pointed to a thick block wall dividing the playground from the street.*

> *"Why?" I asked, naively.*

> *"They be shooting. We are safer there," he replied.*

Because my prior experience filtered the noise as a car backfire, I did not experience the sound in the same manner as the Watts-raised fifth grader.

Because he had already heard many gunshots in his life, his first thought was not of a car backfiring, but that we should take care to protect ourselves.

The kids and I continued our lesson next to the red brick wall; learning BOSS OF YOUR BRAIN, BELLY BREATHING, FIVE SECOND LIGHTSWITCH, WHAT IF?, POSITIVE TWA, and REALITY CHECK and other tools to empower these kids to take control of their lives.

Continued next page

I never learned if it was a gunshot or an automotive glitch, but that is not the point. The point is that we all have unique ways of filtering information and it is almost always based on prior experiences.

When we realize that our beliefs are based, rightly or wrongly, on prior experiences, we have the opportunity to re-think and re-wire our future experiences.

I will not hear a car backfire in the same manner, and am forever altered by my willingness to listen to another human's interpretation.

Coach Taylor

YOU WIN!!!! NEW POSITIVE HABIT FORMED!!!

And, when you support this habit of putting a wedge into the old neurological pathway for 21 days it is likely that you will have given birth to a new, more powerful habit.

If you get thoughts out of the AUTOMATIC THINKING and into the SMART THINKING area consistently for 21 days, it is likely that you will have a new, positive habit, a new way of automatically reacting which serves you better.

TAKE TIME TO REFLECT

What are some good neurological habits that you have developed during your life? Did you know that learning to write or read is done through a neurological pathway?

Learning to run, talk, react, love, or fight are all learned neurological pathways. What neurological habits have you modified while incarcerated?

Awakening at a different time or doing a new job is a new neurological pathway. What neurological habits did you change as you grew from a tiny tot to a young person and then into adulthood?

We all have good and bad habits that are actual neurological pathways in our bodies.

Behaviors that promote smiles in others tend to be supported by good neurological pathways. Behaviors that cause frowns, anger or withdrawal from others are likely to be pathways that you might consider reconstructing.

The truth is, it is likely that you have more GOOD and POSITIVE neurological pathways than bad ones. The problem is that the bad ones, the AUTOMATIC HABITS that get you in trouble usually are given too much control.

Signs of "good" neurological habits or traits include having a sense of humor, a good work ethic, honesty, kindness, love of family, as well as having the ability to pray, or be athletic. Good neurological pathways support growth and positive emotions.

We all are born with a set of good neurological habits. Over time, we develop less productive neurological pathways. Typically, we develop poor neurological pathways as coping tools used to deal with situations that appear beyond our control.

All the positive abilities that you have developed are represented within your body as desirable neurological pathways. Reflect on your good and bad neurological habits. Take a few moments to assess how much of your behavior causes or creates smiles in others. How much of your behavior causes or creates irritation or negative reactions from others? How much of your behavior permits you to smile? How much of your behavior results in positive reactions from others?

Addiction, irrational anger and self-centered attitudes are all negative, unproductive neurological habits. In contrast, integrity, calmness, honesty, honor, freedom from addiction, and patience are examples of good neurological habits.

Remember, every individual has the capability to create new neurological habits. It takes about 21 days of repetitive thoughts and actions to create a new neurological habit inside your body.

Take a moment and think about your own internal wiring. What are some of the neurological habits that you would like to transform?

Do you like to write notes in letters or a journal? You can track your internal changes by documenting your good and bad habits.

For many individuals, writing is a creative process that helps synthesize information and experiences. If you were to write down your good habits and your bad habits, what would you write? With whom would you share this list?

Perhaps now is the time to begin your observation — not just of your internal world, but also the world around you.

OBSERVE OTHERS

Observation of others gives you vital information about your environment and places you in a powerful position of accepting and receiving additional knowledge and information.

You can observe and wonder why someone behaves in a destructive manner. Or you can observe and use the information learned to help you improve your own behavior.

Understanding the behavior and actions of others enables you to control your reactions and environment. As an added benefit, your positive perception will allow you to react more effectively.

You can also learn patterns of behavior from those around you. Being able to predict the behavior of another is a powerful tool for your success.

Just a Thought

No matter what you know, or how smart you are -- you do not know all there is to know.

There will always be new and different and better ways to see things and new information to experience. Because things are always changing, there is always a new way of being.

You are changing, even now, because as a human, you absorb information that your brain places in categories. You then assign a meaning to it, even if there is "no meaning." From that meaning you create your life

Coach Taylor

When observing others, you can see that neurological pathways play out in predictable ways.

When you watch others, you are also subconsciously and automatically measuring yourself and your own options for behavior.

When you observe, you may consider adding the information gleaned from the success and failure of others.

Would you handle the situation in the same manner? Would you react differently? Why is that person reacting in that way?

Heightened awareness

There are as many different ways of reacting as there are circumstances. Some individuals have short fuses. Why? What provokes them?

Notice when they let go of the steering wheel of their life. Do they blame the other driver for their car wreck?

"He made me!" or "It's his fault," are all statements that let a person take their hands off the wheel and let outside forces drive their life.

When you observe others let go of their steering wheel, ask yourself, "are they the boss of their brain or is their brain processing old, thought-less patterns?"

More often than not, when reactions are angry, loud, aggressive, or out of control -- they are not the boss of their brain. They are stuck in AUTOMATIC THINKING.

Coach Taylor as guest lecturer to University Psychology students preparing for probation and other civil service careers in Romania.

CONSIDER THIS...

BOSS OF YOUR BRAIN
is an easy tool for you to
use when you need to take
complete control of your thoughts.

And...

BOSS OF YOUR BRAIN
helps oxygen get to your
muscles so that your body relaxes.
A relaxed body
usually makes
better decisions.

BOSS OF YOUR BRAIN
In Action

MIKE STOPS YELLING

When Mike was a kid, his parents were constantly yelling at each other, at him, at the television or anything that was not meeting their expectations. As a result, Mike learned that he needed to yell loudly to be heard.

Over time, his body developed a neurological habit of yelling which got him into trouble at school, with girlfriends, and he was fired from work more than once. Eventually, his yelling escalated to assault and resisting arrest—a situation that could have easily been avoided.

Mike wanted, and needed, to change. He finally decided to take control of his behavior. He learned to control himself by following the BOSS OF YOUR BRAIN steps.

He practiced this tool of thinking about the wiring of his thoughts several times every day. Sometimes he slipped (relapsed) and reverted back to old neurological habits. But through constant practice, he was also beginning to strengthen a new way to respond. How did Mike learn to be the boss of his brain?

BOSS OF YOUR BRAIN IN ACTION

STEP 1)   INFORMATION IN - Mike's girlfriend tells him she is going out with her friends to a bar instead of seeing him.   This information gets transmitted from Mike's ears to the center of his brain. He automatically goes into his predictable response, his AUTOMATIC THINKING.   A switch along the old neurological pathway gets flipped on, and sends information down the old, worn and unproductive road of yelling.

STEP 2)   ELECTRICAL CURRENT – He knows that his response to her right now is not SMART THINKING; it is a habit, an old habit. He has been down this road before. He starts to yell then he drinks and then he gets locked up for yelling at some stupid bartender who limits his drinks. He does not want this current to play out.

STEP 3)   AUTOMATIC THINKING Mike knows that He does not want the AUTOMATIC THINKING to be the BOSS of him but it seems beyond his control. SHE always makes him mad. It's HER fault.

"How stupid can she be? She always does this," Mike says to himself, as he recounts all the times she has messed up and gotten herself into situations that he ended up trying to fix.

STEP 4)   WEDGE - When the old current began to play out, Mike considers his old way of reacting. It's a habit to yell, but it is not his only option. His most useful WEDGE is walking away.

Even though she is yelling at him as he walks out of the apartment, he keeps walking. It's the only way that he seems to be able to walk away from his AUTOMATIC THINKING and have time to get to his SMART THINKING.

Mike is being the BOSS by not letting his AUTOMATIC THINKING become in charge. He knows he can create new thoughts, SMART THINKING.

Mike put in his most successful WEDGE, he walked away. Now he needs to follow this new road, this alternate current of energy flowing through his body.

"I can't control what you do," he says to his girlfriend in a phone call from his own apartment, "and I am not trying to control you, but just remember your DUI. Remember that your insurance is expensive — you will get locked up, and the car will be impounded again if you are not careful and get pulled over. I don't think it is smart risking everything like that."

Whatever her response might be, Mike begins to build a new neurological habit for himself without yelling. He got the AUTOMATIC THINKING to stop by placing a WEDGE and he moved into SMART THINKING.

How his girlfriend processes his communication and how she responds is not the point. The only thing that matters is that Mike begins to be the boss of his brain and that he gets behind the steering wheel of his life. Mike, and only Mike, can break his yelling habit.

STEP 5)   21 DAYS - It takes 21 days to make a new neurological habit. Mike wants a new way of acting. He wants a new habit of responding. He remembers that only he can make his life better through his new habits. A new habit that he wants to have is being calmer, and handling things more powerfully.

He realizes after 21 days, it becomes almost automatic to respond in a calm manner. By slowing down before reacting, he yells less frequently, he does not get sucked into anyone's drama.

After a while people begin to comment that he seems more calm. Their comments of support serve to reinforce his positive new habits.

Mike eventually finds that the power of changing his behavior through being the boss of his brain is helpful in all areas of his life. He finds that he has developed has successful mastery of reactions; establishing new neurological rivers, which become a new neurological pathway in his body.

WHY IT WORKS

The human body is pretty simple to control when you understand how the body operates. You can decide to be the BOSS OF YOUR BRAIN.

What keeps us from changing bad habits? Fear. Fear of failure. Lazy. Too lazy to stick out the process of change. Low self esteem. Not believing in yourself enough to know, deep down, that you can make your life powerfully good.

BOSS OF YOUR BRAIN provides the tools for you to be the boss, to get in the driver's seat, take control, and get rid of unproductive neurological pathways.

You can completely control your actions and reactions when you fully master the concept of BOSS OF YOUR BRAIN.

BOSS OF YOUR BRAIN
In Action

STEVE AND ANGER

Steve had a problem with his anger. His mother always yelled at him when she got angry, telling Steve that he was just like his father. His father had a problem with anger, especially when he was drinking.

Steve felt like he would never be able to change and that he was destined to be angry most of the time. Thoughts came into his mind that he could not seem to control.

When he got angry, he often acted in ways that he regretted. He wished that he would not get so angry, but when his thoughts took over, he could not seem to stop them.

Besides, Steve thought that people were basically irritating and they got on his nerves a lot. Steve got irritated easily and blew up at the slightest provocation.

He felt out of control when his anger took over. Since both his parents angered easily, Steve thought that he had no choice but to get angry as well. He even got angry with himself for getting angry!

THINK ABOUT IT

How would Steve use the techniques of BOSS OF YOUR BRAIN to help him with his anger?

What actions will Steve need to put into practice to do BOSS OF YOUR BRAIN?

STEP 1) INFORMATION IN - Information comes into the very center of Steve's brain for processing through his sense of sight, smell, touch, hearing and taste. He begins his AUTOMATIC THINKING, using habits tucked in the back of his brain.

STEP 2) ELECTRICAL CURRENT - Much like an electrical current, this information shoots through Steve's body with a meaning attached. Steve has created these meaning based on his prior experiences and expectations for the future. Because Steve is a human, he naturally and automatically gives meaning to the information that he experiences. Remember, Steve decides what things mean based on previous experiences and future expectations.

STEP 3) AUTOMATIC THINKING - When the old current of meaning begins to flow his AUTOMATIC THINKING begins to take over. Steve remembers the parts of the brain and he takes the control.   He remembers BOSS OF YOUR BRAIN.

STEP 4)   WEDGE – Steve knows that the only thing that can save him is if she gets his thoughts to be SMART THINKING rather than AUTOMATIC THINKING. For Steve, his WEDGE is calling a friend. He pulls out his phone and starts to dial. Sometimes just pulling out his phone is enough. Even leaving a message is helpful. He just needs a WEDGE to give him time to get his thinking into SMART THINKING.

Once Steve starts his SMART THINKING he is starting to "rewire" his physical neurology. He is actually building an alternate current of meaning. This alternate current of meaning is going to naturally modify Steve's reactions and actions.

STEP 5)   21 DAYS - It takes about 21 days to replace an old habit and make a new neurological habit.

Steve needs to remember…
Sometimes lasting change happens slowly. He just keeps moving forward.

THIS WEEK'S CHALLENGE

OBSERVE OTHERS...

Spend a little time observing the bad habits that control the life experiences of the individuals around you.

Neurological habits run the behavior of guards, staff, cell mates, friends, family, employers and yourself. Everyone runs old, worn neurological habits.

Just observe and let behavior tell you about the habits of others. Let their habits tell you if they are the boss and in the driver's seat of their life, or if their brain is running on a tank full of negative habits.

Also, observe yourself...

Notice when you are BOSS OF YOUR BRAIN. Can you begin to build new neurological habits? Which are the habitual pathways you would most benefit from rewiring, or reconstructing?

GOGI Supporters & Friends

Reverend/Doctor Mara Leigh "Coach" Taylor at her ordination next to her mentor, Father Giles and daughter, Mia, in New York City.

Sita, Coach Taylor, author Gloria Karpinski and Bo Lozoff.

CHAPTER FIVE

BELLY BREATHING

Words from a brother...
  Belly Breathing sounds funny because it is funny. How you gunna tell a "G" that belly breathing is powerful? But, check it out. Filling your belly area with air calms you down and you become relaxed. The muscles need the oxygen. Especially when you are nervous, the first thing you do is take a deep breath.
  Don't trip on the name, trip on the effect of Belly Breathing. With practice, you'll be doing it when you don't even know you are doing it. Your brain needs oxygen and when you give it more oxygen your thinking doesn't rebel against you. So you're more relaxed.
  Especially when you're nervous, the first thing you do is Belly Breathing.

Use this tool in the process of empowering yourself to make strong and solid decisions — to run your own life in a powerful manner.

If you read the entire book too quickly, you cannot possibly benefit as much as those individuals who focus on each concept for a full week. Remember to take your time and truly integrate the ideas into daily activities.

The secret of making these tools work for you is to work on the tools. Practice them and integrate them into your daily life.

Practice the skill of BOSS OF YOUR BRAIN and you will begin to put the concepts into action automatically. Re-read and focus your efforts in the mastery of the first and most important component of your foundation—understanding and integrating the concepts of BOSS OF YOUR BRAIN.

This component is designed to help get you into the driver's seat, to give you control over your decisions and actions. You will be at the mercy of others until you realize that you can control your actions.

Take control of your life...

BOSS OF YOUR BRAIN was designed as an easy way to empower you to take control of your life.

Practice the BOSS OF YOUR BRAIN tool until you have a solid grasp on the power to re-direct and actually create new thoughts. Then the other tools will help you reach your potential level of freedom.

You can think that you know all the tricks in the book. But if you do not know - deep down inside - that you are in charge of your own life - you are never completely free.

GOGI is a California-based non-profit organization serving at risk and incarcerated individuals. GETTING OUT BY GOING IN teaches psychology students the simple concepts of the curriculum in preparation for their volunteer work as GOGI coaches.

After they are taught the concept of BOSS OF YOUR BRAIN, they are given the tool of BELLY BREATHING. They are taught how to breathe only after they learn that they are the boss of their brain. Until they are in the driver's seat, it is not as powerful to have them breathing properly.

When you know that you are BOSS OF YOUR BRAIN and you breathe powerfully, you are able to consciously move oxygen throughout your body.

When you consciously move oxygen throughout your body, your brain gets the adequate oxygen for making positive decisions.

Don't let your brain betray you

It is less likely that your brain will betray you when you are in control of your thoughts and reactions. Breathe powerfully. When you are the boss, enough oxygen gets into to your brain to let it operate powerfully.

Your brain will only betray you when it is not under your control and when you forfeit your right to think and react in a manner that empowers you.

The tools of BOSS OF YOUR BRAIN and BELLY BREATHING are designed to get you back in control. And for many of you, it may be the first time you have been in control.

Many individuals come out of the womb in an environment void of basic tools of self-empowerment and positive decision-making. Does this sound familiar? Perhaps your parents never taught you because they never learned the tools themselves.

Without information, how are you to learn? Self-empowerment is not taught in schools. It is often taught in sports or churches, but increasing numbers of individuals do not take advantage of these resources.

No more excuses

Now, however, you have no excuse. You can no longer blame your parents, society, or the system. You can no longer abdicate your right to create your own life and your personal internal freedom — because these tools are simple enough to use and fit into your daily life.

The GOGI tools are even taught to kindergarten children with great success. Of course, you can learn them. Of course, you can be successful.

Just keep reading and rereading. Keep practicing and practicing some more.

The Clinical Combined with Experience

The tools of BOSS OF YOUR BRAIN and BELLY BREATHING are linked. Knowing you are the BOSS OF YOUR BRAIN permits you to do BELLY BREATHING in a manner which leads to optimal decision making. The tools are delivered clinically and in psychological terms and through the voice of experience.

Coach DJ's prison experience is combined with psychological schooling and volunteer work with prisoners. When combined, the clinical and the experience, a full picture is presented for you to integrate the two. It enables you, the reader, to see how to integrate clinical concepts directly into your life through the example set by another.

Coach DJ succinctly said, "When you do BELLY BREATHING your brain WILL NOT BETRAY YOU."

This is a voice of experience sharing with you a truth. And when you know the psychological concepts behind his first-hand knowledge experience, you may integrate this truth into your very being. His simple statement, "When you do BELLY BREATHING your brain WILL NOT BETRAY YOU," was a synthesis of academic learning blended with the truth revealed through experience.

Please do not limit your opportunities by being put off by the academic approach to some of these concepts. Begin to widen your learning. Entertain the idea that you can read something academic and create your own experience.

> *Combine the academic with your personal experience. Make these concepts yours and then write us at: GOGI, PO Box 88969, Los Angeles, CA 90009 USA so that we might share your experience with others.*
>
> *Successful students, after all, are the finest teachers. Your experiences with these concepts will enlighten and teach others.* ☺
>
> *Coach Taylor*

Practice the concept of truly being in the driver's seat of your thoughts and behaviors.

Once you begin to grasp the power inherent in these concepts then begin to talk about them and teach them. One way to really learn something is to talk about it and begin to teach what you have learned.

All the while, pay attention to your own ways of behaving. Really watch yourself operate and see where you do (and don't) have mastery.

Once you have completed the mastery of BOSS OF YOUR BRAIN, then and only then, should you be moving on to the concept of BELLY BREATHING.

Assuming that you have practiced BOSS OF YOUR BRAIN, let's move on to the next level of getting you in control of your life.

You will learn about another powerful tool for improving your life. It is a very simple tool called:

"BELLY BREATHING"

The most powerful tools that we have as individuals are often the most simple.

You would think that breathing is natural, and that it is done correctly and automatically. However, this is not the case. You may also think that breathing properly is not very important. However, it is the most important thing that we can do for controlling our thoughts and automatic reactions.

When observing a baby's breathing, you will see his or her entire body expand and contract with every breath. You will see their belly rise and fall as they effortlessly take in oxygen.

As you watch them, it seems as if their entire body fills with air because their little body expands and moves with every breath. It seems as if their entire body contracts and moves with every breath when the unused air is exhaled. This can be compared to a balloon as it moves and expands when it is filled with air.

Take it from the little ones...

To breathe as effortlessly as a baby does is the natural process of breathing. If you observe adults, however, you will see a wide variety of breathing patterns. Most breathing patterns of adults are ineffectual at relieving stress. In some cases, breathing can provoke anxiety or rage.

You might notice that individuals who are stressed, chronically depressed, angry, or irritated have a breathing pattern that is very different from those who are relaxed and calm.

The calm person's body moves and expands when they breathe. The uptight person's body is likely to remain rigid and stiff, as the air has a difficult time getting into the lungs.

A chronically angry person may attempt to become still and quiet. Yet, it is very likely that when he breathes, his chest will rise and fall rapidly. The shoulders of stressed individuals might noticeably rise and fall with every breath.

Some individuals might appear to have no signs of breathing, as their body is so rigid and stressed that it is barely moves. Stressed, angry or fearful individuals fall into the habit of breathing poorly.

When an individual is breathing properly, the belly area will move in and out with every breath.

In stressed individuals, sometimes the belly will not move at all.

FIGHT OR FLIGHT RESPONSE

Breathing automatically becomes rapid and localized in the chest area during the state of anger, fear, danger, or heightened physiological awareness. Shallow breathing is a physiological response to the need to

BELLY BREATHING   ◀131▶

pump oxygen quickly into your lungs in response to immediate danger. This quick-fix response to danger does not support the body's long-term success at relaxation.

When breathing rapidly, your body instantly enters a "Fight or Flight" response. The body is designed to react automatically to threats or impending danger.

It is necessary for the logical part of the brain to shut down and let your animal instincts take over when threatened with the loss of life.

As the body enters a panicked state with shallow and rapid breathing, the "smart," or logical thinking shuts down. It automatically signals you to "fight for your life" or "take flight" and run to safety. This natural reaction is called the "Fight or Flight Response."

Breathing so that air only gets into the chest is "shallow" breathing and a natural defense mechanism designed to help you protect yourself when you need to act quickly to save your life.

Although it may help under threatening circumstances, this type of shallow or limited chest breathing can be disadvantageous in relationships.

You are smarter, calmer, and more powerful and able to make better decisions when you breathe in a relaxed manner. The angry, depressed, irritated individual usually utilizes chest breathing. The entire body is missing out on much needed oxygen.

THE LIMBIC SYSTEM

Let's look at an area inside the brain called the limbic system. The limbic system is a group of brain parts that has many functions. One important job is to warn us when we are in situations of real or perceived danger.

When we believe that we are in danger, the limbic system sends out messages and our body reacts immediately.

When we are anxious, angry, fearful, depressed or have similar emotions, it is likely that our limbic system is pumping cortisol into our blood system in amounts that alter our reactions.

High levels of cortisol can be counter productive

Cortisol is valuable as it gives us the ability to react to stressful situations in an immediate and urgent manner.

Cortisol has an important function in your body. However, it is not useful when individuals experience or interpret an environment to be hostile. That is when it delivered throughout the body constantly and continually.

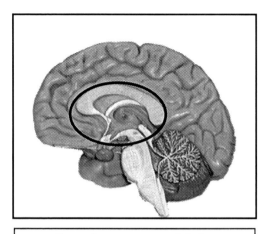

The Limbic System is circled above.

When too much cortisol pumps throughout your system, or when other hormones and chemicals are out of balance, the signs become observable in the body.

Individuals with tightly balled fists are usually operating from a stress-based, high cortisol-level way of being. Individuals with cold hands and feet, extra weight around their middle, shallow breathing are all likely to be suffering from high levels of stress and high levels of cortisol.

It is interesting to note that when we get used to this type of functioning it becomes a neurological pathway and the body assumes it as a normal habit.

When we are stressed for a long enough period of time our body thinks, "Ok. This is how I am supposed to be. Stress is the natural state. Let me just settle into pumping out more cortisol and tightening up my muscles."

We might exist with high levels of cortisol and other "fight or flight" responses and think that it is normal. In some cases, we DO live in environments that are potentially dangerous and therefore our bodies are never given the opportunity to know what it is like to be physically at peace.

The truth of the matter

The truth of the matter is that the body was designed to breathe like a baby, with each and every part of the body gently expanding and contracting as we calmly inhale and exhale.

BELLY BREATHING is a technique that works instantly on even the most habitual chest or shoulder breathing. This breathing technique is important for those having a difficult time controlling negative or unproductive thoughts or actions.

Scientific studies prove that breathing properly relaxes the mind and increases the likelihood that thoughts and actions can be controlled.

BELLY BREATHING will:

- Help Improve Thoughts and Feelings of Anger
- Decrease Sadness
- Decrease Loneliness
- Decrease Rage
- Decrease Depression
- Decrease Helplessness
- Decrease Grief
- Help Alleviate Addiction
- Increased Good Health
- Increase Optimism
- Increase Happiness

BELLY BREATHING – the legit shortcut to self-empowerment and enlightenment.

The People of GOGI

Coach Felicia poses with Inglewood City Chief of Police at an event honoring Inglewood's volunteers.

Backward Breathing

Federal prison inmate DJ Verrett was one of 35 inmates on the GOGI weekly call-out in 2005. He'd quietly stroll into class and listen, never commenting, never judging. Like many other course participants, he would observe how others reacted to what was being said. Basically, he was in that group of participants who observed and remained open to learning new ways to create a powerful life.

Whenever DJ participated, I observed that his breathing did not empower him to make good decisions nor did his way of breathing calm him and permit his brain to make positive decisions automatically. When he inhaled his stomach contracted, it sucked inward, and his shoulders lifted. When he exhaled, his shoulders dropped and his stomach expanded. This is not optimal breathing.

Optimal breathing is when the belly expands as it fills up with air.

DJ mastered BELLY BREATHING quickly because he was also taking other supportive courses like meditation, reading, and exploring different ways that helped him empower his life. Upon his release, he began to dedicate all his free time to volunteer work, teaching at risk kids the GOGI concepts.

When I witnessed "Coach" DJ in front of an audience of stressed-out, at-risk kids and saw him teach the value of getting oxygen into their brains, I knew that there is no better teacher than the student who recognizes that his body needs a little oxygen to make positive decisions. It was from getting oxygen to his body that finally gave him SPACE to do things differently.

> *How many of you can integrate what you have learned behind bars to eventually empower youth to create positive choices?*
>
> *How many of you can begin to be a positive influence to other incarcerated individuals? How many of you will reach beyond the bars to your families and friends? What can you do today to share positive tools with others?*
>
> *Coach Taylor*

HOW DOES BELLY BREATHING WORK?

When you use **BELLY BREATHING**, oxygen flows into the lungs more effectively and your body is relaxed enough to process the oxygen optimally. Breathing this way allows your body to relax. Relaxed breathing allows you to make better decisions and handle adverse situations better.

ADDED BENEFITS OF BELLY BREATHING

There is an additional benefit to the **BELLY BREATHING** technique. When breathing with the stomach area, the muscles in that area become firmer and stronger. This is the kind of breathing that athletes use in their regular exercise regime to build strong, lean muscles in their stomach area.

THE TRUTH IS. . .

BELLY BREATHING
allows your entire body
to become more relaxed.
A relaxed body
is inclined to make
more positive and
powerful decisions.

Mastering **BELLY BREATHING** in every day life allows you to react differently to stress. An extra bonus can be to develop a firmer set of stomach muscles in the process.

The People of GOGI

Coach Sharai speaking to a group of kids at a Compton, California school.

HERE'S WHY BELLY BREATHING WORKS...

When you are angry, fearful, or in a state of rage, it is possible that you are breathing with limited oxygen into the lungs.

It is likely that you will begin breathing with your chest rising and falling. Your belly is likely to remain still. "Chest breathing" limits the amount of oxygen available throughout your body.

Can you tell if you are BELLY BREATHING or chest breathing as you read? Reading is usually a relaxing activity and it could be that your belly expands and contract during this relaxed state.

How are you breathing right this very moment? Is your belly rising and falling with each breath?

When there is limited oxygen in the body, you cannot fully function. With limited oxygen, "smart" decisions get put to the side and "emergency" or "panic" decisions move into panic actions. Panic decisions are rarely your best decisions.

HOW TO DO <u>BELLY BREATHING</u>

If you can control your thoughts, you can control your actions. And you can control the way you respond to the actions of others.

An action is always preceded by a thought, even when we are not aware of the thought. A major tool in controlling your thoughts is simply getting oxygen to the entire brain and throughout your entire body.

As simple as it seems, BELLY BREATHING and the act of getting the proper amount of oxygen to the entire body is likely to change your actions when you are angry or upset.

Here are the three simple steps for BELLY BREATHING.

STEP 1) SOLID GROUND - No matter what is going on, think about how firmly your feet are on the ground. Think about placing them firmly on the earth as you begin the process of BELLY BREATHING. Plant your feet on solid ground. People are usually better breathers if they feel solid.

STEP 2) FILL YOUR FEET - One way that helps individuals who are really stuck in bad breathing patterns is to have them pretend and use their imagination. If you are having a difficult time getting effortless breath into your lungs so that your body will process that oxygen optimally, here is a little trick that works wonders on the most difficult or tense individuals.

Imagine for a moment that you need to fill your feet up with air. Imagine that your lungs, which are in your chest area, are actually in your feet. It might seem funny to pretend that your lungs are actually located in your feet; but this technique works wonders at getting the body prepared for optimal breathing.

Imagine that your feet expand and contract like two balloons filling up with air each time you breathe. This trick works perfectly to help the body do what it is designed to do and get fresh oxygen into the entire blood stream.

The People
of
GOGI

Coach Sharai teaches Belly Breathing to GOGI youth.

STEP 3) BELLY BREATHE - Fill your stomach area like a balloon as you inhale. When you inhale, imagine that there is a balloon in your belly and as you take in air the balloon expands. The more you inhale air the bigger the belly-balloon gets.

When exhaling, see if you can pull your belly button to your spine. If you are not certain you are doing it properly, try this trick before you fall asleep. Lay on your back. Place a book or your hand over your belly button. Just observe.

Do nothing but feel what happens as the air moves in and out of your body. Take some time and just watch your belly area.

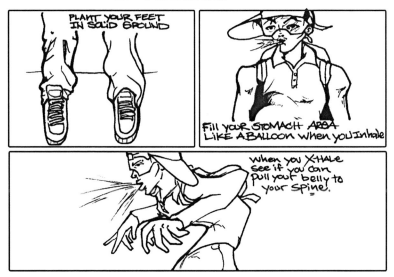

As you inhale, notice that when air comes into your body, your lungs fill up and your belly fills up. Likewise, when air leaves your body, watch as your hand on your belly moves lower toward your spine.

Keep doing this, night after night. You will become aware of a new breathing pattern that will soon extend into the daylight hours. BELLY BREATHING will help you master relaxed breathing.

THINK ABOUT IT

Sometimes individuals get so angry that they make bad decisions or act in ways that they would not normally behave. When your body is running its own program and automatically reacting from high levels of cortisol, it may seem impossible to STOP the anger or the unproductive thought or feeling.

Do you remember a time when you were so angry or afraid that it seemed as if your body just took over? All of us "lost control" of our actions or reactions at one time or another. When you lost control, did you react in a way that was unproductive or harmful to yourself or others?

Take a moment to observe how you are breathing right at this moment. Does your chest move when you breathe? Does your stomach move up and down when you breathe? Does your chest and stomach move at the same time? Do your shoulders move? Do you have control over your breathing? Can you selectively move your chest or your stomach when you breathe?

Go easy on yourself

Go easy on yourself when learning this and all self-empowerment techniques. Remember, sometimes lasting change happens slowly and over time. You may also be working on "bad" habits that you've had for a long time.

Lastly, give change an honest chance and keep practicing. Eventually, your body will create the new habit that will serve to your advantage. You may not even notice the changes. That does not matter. Just keep moving forward. It takes about 21 days to create a new neurological habit inside your body. Keep practicing week after week and before you know it, you will have created a new neurological habit for yourself.

And remember, too, that somewhere very early in your childhood you developed habits due to your experiences and environment. You might have heard gunshots on a playground that frightened you. Like the 5th grader in Watts, California, you may have developed a physiological coping tool that caused you to breathe from a state of fear.

The good news is the fact that you can change how your body responds to almost anything. Continue to practice BOSS OF YOUR BRAIN and BELLY BREATHING. They work to assist you in the changes that will undoubtedly improve your life.

WATCH OTHERS

Observation of others will give you vital information and place you in a powerful position of knowledge. Just observe individuals when they get angry. Watch how they are breathing. You might notice that most people's breathing gets short and shallow when they are in a state of anger or rage. Their fists might ball up, face get red, and actions become abrupt and forceful. When people breathe this way, they are not relaxed and they are not making the smartest decisions.

You will know if someone is breathing poorly if you can see their chest rise and fall when they breathe. If a person is doing the BELLY BREATHING, their chest will remain still and the stomach area will go in and out with every breath.

CONSIDER THIS...

> ### BELLY BREATHING
>
> *is an easy tool for*
>
> *you to use when you need*
>
> *to take complete control*
>
> *of your body.*
>
> ### BELLY BREATHING
>
> *helps to relax your body*
>
> *to allow you access to*
>
> *better decision making skills.*

BELLY BREATHING
In Action

MIKE QUITS SMOKING WEED

Mike, 27, has smoked weed with his brothers since he was 9 years old. All his troubles still seem to go away for a while when he is loaded.

He has been clean for two weeks now, but he is more irritable and angry than usual. Mike and his girl broke up a few days ago and he is thinking that he should call her and see if they can work it out.

He goes over to his buddy's house to think about things. He is greeted by several people that he knows and they are partying and having a good time. As if that wasn't enough to make him start smoking again, the worst part of it is the fact that his girlfriend is sitting on the couch just a bit too close to one of his best friends. His thoughts run wild and he wants to strike out at his girlfriend and his friend.

To let the BELLY BREATHING work for him, Mike needs to take control. He remembers that he knows how to do the BELLY BREATHING, which is his tool to use any time he wants to take control of a situation and do things differently.

He remembers the steps to BELLY BREATHING. No matter how mad he is at his girlfriend, he knows he is the boss of his brain and that his life is up to him. He puts the BELLY BREATHING into action.

BELLY BREATHING IN ACTION

1) **SOLID GROUND** - Mike feels his feet firmly on the ground. He lets himself feel more solid with both feet firmly on the ground. He can be very firm about what is good for him and what he wants to do when he feels solid. Mike is committed to himself to quit smoking weed—he is solid and wants to be strong.

2) **FILL THE FEET** - Mike imagines what it would be like if his lungs are in his feet and he breathes as if he must fill up his feet with air. This is an easy way to get oxygen throughout his body. His body relaxes a little. He can remember what he wants with his life. He is the boss and in control of his thoughts and actions.

He feels solid and strong when he gets breath all the way to his feet. Breathing this way permits him to be firm about his commitment to quit smoking weed.

3) BELLY BREATHE - Mike turns his focus to his stomach area. He takes a deep breath and lets his stomach expand like a balloon filling up with air. When he exhales, he pulls his belly button tightly inward toward his spine.

When Mike breathes this way, it allows his entire body to relax. He has a better focus on his goals and does not let anyone or anything pull him off track when his body relaxes.

WHY IT WORKS

BELLY BREATHING helps move oxygen throughout Mike's body. When Mike gets air throughout his body, it places him in a more relaxed state. Mike can think smartly when he is relaxed and he remembers that he has control over his thoughts and actions.

He makes better decisions when he is relaxed. He can now think BEYOND the immediate situation and into the future with BELLY BREATHING.

He can avoid thoughts and actions that would take him away from what he really wants. He is learning that he can focus on positive outcomes that will bring peace of mind.

OBSERVE OTHERS...

Observe others and their breathing patterns. Notice guards who have shallow breathing. Pay attention to individuals coming out of chapel or yoga class. Do they breathe differently? Who is uptight and who is relaxed? How does their breathing pattern betray their truth?

In a short amount of time, just by observing someone's breathing patterns, you may begin to predict if they are going "lose it" or if they are dealing resourcefully in a situation.

Also, observe yourself...

Notice when you are BELLY BREATHING. Does your stomach rise and fall with every breath? Can you move the breathing from your chest to your stomach and back again? Take notice of who is in charge of your body's breathing if and when you lose control.

The People of GOGI

GOGI Coach Wanda works with at-risk kids in elementary, middle and high schools. Certified Coaches teach at-risk kids how to be Boss of Your Brain.

TOOLS FOR THE MIND

CHAPTER SIX
FIVE SECOND LIGHTSWITCH

Words from a brother...

My lightswitch is that I am able to find a comfort zone with in five seconds. It could be a childhood memory, something positive that I am doing that I bring to mind. I think about where I am headed. My goals. My destructive thoughts only last a moment. I turn on the lightswitch to another thought.

I messed up so many good moments because I let old thoughts run my program. Now I am the BOSS and I turn on the lightswitch to how I want my life to be. I hit the lightswitch and it's all good.

Don't get me wrong, I am challenged on a daily basis but I have the tools to correct it. All it takes is a few seconds.

The process of internal freedom comes in steps toward your self-empowerment. The steps are similar to building a house. You cannot paint the walls before laying the foundation. The first two tools: BOSS OF YOUR BRAIN and BELLY BREATHING lay the foundation for lasting and profound change.

Make certain you have a firm grasp of the concepts presented and that you are able to use them fairly effortlessly. It is absolutely fine, normal and expected if it takes you longer than one week to completely "get" a concept.

Some GOGI students take up to a month to grasp the idea that they are the boss, and that their brain is under control. Others take weeks and weeks to relearn how to breathe properly.

While some people say they understand a concept, they may still blame everyone else for their situation.

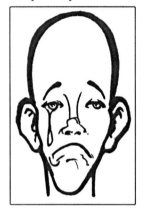

This is not a firm foundation from which to empower your life. This is not freedom. It is actually abdicating power by handing the driving wheel over to the person who made you upset.

By taking total responsibility for your life, these tools will become powerfully effective. When you are ready, and feel as if BOSS OF YOUR BRAIN and BELLY BREATHING are easy, then and only then should you add FIVE SECOND LIGHTSWITCH.

FIVE SECOND LIGHTSWITCH may challenge everything you have learned about breaking bad habits.

It is likely you have been told, "Don't think about it," or "Put it out of your mind," when you are confronted with the temptation to return to an old, worn and undesirable behavior.

It is not easy for individuals to walk away from old habits, or ways of behaving or thinking. It takes a rare individual to walk away from a bad habit without a struggle – I offer congratulations to those who can.

Many people, however, need to gradually incorporate new habits and realities when processing change. The FIVE SECOND LIGHTSWITCH is an easy tool for breaking bad habits because it acknowledges that all thoughts are powerful.

The **FIVE SECOND LIGHTSWITCH** will help you:

- Take control of thoughts that are bad habits.

- Take control of feelings that you cannot "get away" from your bad habit.

- Take control of actions that result from your thoughts and feelings.

The People of GOGI

Coach Taylor working with kids in the GOGI SIGN UP FOR SUCCESS! program.

THE TRUTH IS. . .

FIVE SECOND LIGHTSWITCH
*will allow you to work WITH
your mind instead of against it.*

FIVE SECOND LIGHTSWITCH
*will allow you to
experience your ability
to control your actions.*

FIVE SECOND LIGHTSWITCH
*will permit distance from
disabling habits
and empower you to
change other behaviors as well.*

HOW DOES THE LIGHTSWITCH WORK?

When you try to stop thinking about your temper, it seems that all you can think about is your temper.

When you try to stop thinking about your soon-to-be ex-wife and your divorce, it seems that all you can think about is your soon-to-be ex-wife and your divorce.

When you are trying to lose weight and you tell yourself not to think about food, it seems that all you can think about is food.

Most of the time, telling yourself to stop a thought just isn't going to work. Sometimes, in fact, it has an opposite effect.

FIVE SECOND LIGHTSWITCH is effective because it works on the belief that your thoughts are like rivers of information flowing through your body.

You can stop a river by frantically building a dam to stop its flow. Or, you can gently divert the water and let it run in another direction.

FIVE SECOND LIGHTSWITCH gently redirects the water towards a better, more productive flow.

HERE'S WHY THE LIGHTSWITCH WORKS...

FIVE SECOND LIGHTSWITCH works because most people have a difficult time "stopping" but oftentimes have an easier experience "replacing." The Five Second Lightswitch is a "wedge" placed in the current flow of neurons and sending information down another, more productive path.

Ask a child to stop a behavior and it is likely that they will continue. Their focus is on the undesirable behavior — they don't know what to do as a replacement for it, or how to promote positive actions.

When you divert a child's attention to something else, you are stopping the undesirable behavior.

In the following example the mother gave Joey something to move toward, something more productive to do with his energy and focus.

Giving yourself something else to do with your thoughts is why FIVE SECOND LIGHTSWITCH works.

"I want the cash. I need money! Hmmm. Wait a second. The cash is cool, but do I really want to spend more time in the Pen?"

Joey and the Hot Pan

"Joey, don't touch the pan. It's hot," the mom blurts out to her 3 year old son who is reaching up to the pan handle sticking out from the stove that is directly above his head.

Joey hears the warning but his focus is on grabbing the pan handle. More attention is given to the pan by hearing its name — so even when she says "don't," his mind is still focused on the pan.

Joey then has to include both what his mom said about the pan and the word "don't" in his analysis of the communication. Sometimes we focus on one portion of the communication but fail to remember the "don't" part.

Joey's hand reaches up for the pan.

"Joey, I told you, don't touch that pan," his mom yells louder. "You bad boy. You never listen to me."

Poor Joey is left standing there crying and confused, with a pan full of food splattered all over mom's clean floor.

<u>Joey and the Hot Pan – The Remix</u>

Joey toddles over to the pan area. Seeing pending danger, the mom gently diverts his attention.

"Joey? Hey, look at this," his mom says, holding her fork up in the air with her mashed potatoes balanced expertly.

"Can you help me put these potatoes in my mouth?"

Joey automatically toddles over to where his mother has placed his focus. He helps mom put the fork in her mouth, he feels an increase in personal value and self esteem and mom doesn't need to mop the floor.

"You are so smart, Joey," the mom says.

Now she can personally take him to the stove and explain why she moves the handle from his reach.

"This is very hot. It hurts to touch things that are hot," she tells him.

HOW THE LIGHTSWITCH WORKS

Instead of attempting to immediately STOP the river of thoughts leading to undesirable behavior, let's see if THE FIVE SECOND LIGHTSWITCH is an easier way for you to take control of your life.

THE <u>FIVE SECOND LIGHTSWITCH</u>

STEP 1) THOUGHTS ENTER - A thought enters your mind. "I really wish I could have just one cigarette right now. I really need it, I am so stressed." Or, "I will go back for seconds of this meal; it is actually pretty good, for once." Or, "She makes me so mad. The only times that she listens is when I get angry."

STEP 2) PERMISSION GRANTED - Instead of being upset that you are reverting back to old thoughts, permit those thoughts to toss around in your head for a few seconds. There was a time when those old thoughts served you well by making you feel temporarily better, more powerful, safer, stronger….whatever...

You need to permit the THOUGHT (not the action) to exist for a FULL FIVE SECONDS. Ask yourself, "It served me once but no longer serves me to think this way. Why am I thinking that particular thought?" In those five seconds, think about how the old behavior worked for you. "Cigarettes calmed me down when nothing else would." Or, "If I don't eat now, who knows when I will get something that tastes good." Or, "When I got angry it seemed like she listened more."

STEP 3) THOUGHT SWAP - For five full seconds you have considered all the old benefits of the old behavior. When you get to the sixth second, swap the thought to something, anything leading you away from the old behavior. It's like turning on a light switch and heading the neurons in a more productive direction – a direction that is completely under your control.

"Cigarettes calm me, however: 1) they are expensive, 2) they will shorten my life, and 3) they are a sign of weakness. I will be healthier, smell better and be stronger by not smoking. " Or, "The food tastes good but having my pants fit better is a better idea." or, "While she listens to me when I am angry, for my own sanity I need to communicate in another way. I will not let her control my anger level."

STEP 4) REPEAT REPEAT REPEAT - If the bad habit thought comes back after the sixth second you will repeat, repeat, repeat the process of FIVE SECOND LIGHTSWITCH, reminding yourself of the new direction you are taking with your thoughts and actions. Eventually, the thought about the bad habit will be overruled by the unrelenting persistence of the new thought. If you keep this up long enough, FIVE SECOND LIGHTSWITCH will become automatic and, eventually, you will have a new ways of thinking.

Your biggest challenge might be to maintain the change. In the equation for change explained earlier in this book, DATA (information) needs to be combined with SPACE (time and room for change) and then a SHIFT occurs. This results in changes.

The part of the process that may get discouraging is when the external environment or our own internal environment does not provide enough SPACE for the change to hold.

HOW NEURONS WORK

We learned with BOSS OF YOUR BRAIN that neurons are message holders and that neurotransmitters are the delivery service of the messages.

To change a bad habit the neurons need to transport a new message. The neurotransmitter needs to be told to take the new messages to a new and different place resulting in new and different emotions and actions. FIVE SECOND LIGHTSWITCH helps you accomplish this task.

The key to FIVE SECOND LIGHTSWITCH is that you must repeat and repeat and repeat the process until the new neurological pathways are secured.

New thoughts are like a wedge, leading thoughts in a different direction toward success. Keep putting wedge after wedge in and eventually the neurological river will get the idea that you are no longer feeding the bad habit. It WILL automatically follow your new directions – in about 21 days.

Freeway traffic is easily diverted

It is easier to redirect traffic on a freeway than to stop traffic altogether. The neurology of your body is similar to traffic on a freeway. If you want cars to travel down a different road, you are going to have to put up a roadblock to move the traffic in the desired direction.

You need to be persistent in swapping the thought. Eventually, the traffic will get the idea that the old freeway is not going to be traveled.

When you break an old habit, you have actually created an alternate neurological pathway, or "freeway" of communication inside your body.

Permitting the old thought to exist for five full seconds, and then consciously replacing it with another thought, is like diverting traffic instead of trying to stop it head on. Stopping an entire freeway of traffic is not easy, but getting drivers to take a new off-ramp is much more effective because it is less stressful, demanding, causes fewer collisions and promotes a smoother transition.

THINK ABOUT IT

What habits have you attempted to stop "cold turkey?" If you didn't quite accomplish your goal, ask yourself if the FIVE SECOND LIGHTSWITCH would have been a better option for you.

When you take the opportunity to really consider your thought process, you are actually creating opportunities for change. The more you consider alternatives in behavior the more likely that you will be to begin to test them out.

Remember, everyone has automatic actions and reactions that they would like to change. Oftentimes, it seems difficult to change these habits. So we accept having a temper, eating improperly, being lazy, getting jealous, or stealing as just the way that we are "wired." We begin to accept that the undesirable behavior is unmanageable or "just who we are."

The FIVE SECOND LIGHTSWITCH is another powerful tool for you to use when beginning to reconstruct your internal wiring.

You now have BOSS OF YOUR BRAIN, BELLY BREATHING and the FIVE SECOND LIGHTSWITCH to help you in the process of creating new and positive neurological pathways.

You may go easy on yourself in this process of taking control of your life and implementing lasting change. You have undoubtedly been responding and reacting in ways that have been familiar for quite some time. It will take a while to get just as familiar with new ways of thinking and being. Don't give up.

Change sometimes takes a while

Remember that sometimes lasting change happens slowly and may take a long time — especially when we break or change old habits by replacing them with new ways of thinking, behaving or believing.

Sometimes change is so slow that we don't even know it is happening. Trust the process and just keep moving forward.

Usually, those who are consistent with slow and steady changes are more successful at maintaining those changes over time. They keep moving forward, even if they mess up, and are likely to be happier and more successful in the long haul.

When an individual constantly moves, toward new ways of thinking and being, it is likely that the changes will last for a long time.

- How would the FIVE SECOND LIGHTSWITCH work for you?
- What would be the automatic thoughts that you would want to change?
- How would your life be different?

One step at a time

One habit, one way of thinking at a time will permit you to master your changes in small doses. Focus on wiring one room at a time, instead of trying to re-wire an entire house all at once.

Individuals often become over-enthusiastic. They set their expectations too high and suddenly become overwhelmed. They get irritated and blame an ineffective process for their failure. Some people simply claim that they are different, that they cannot change, have tried everything, or that they really did not want to change in the first place.

The process of change is actually predictable. When DATA or information is available, the process of change begins. When there is enough SPACE for the information to grow into new ideas and new thoughts, then the process of change continues with a SHIFT. When CHANGE happens and it is sustained for a long enough period to form a habit within the body, the process of change has completed its cycle.

Everyone can change how they think, how they act, how they react and how they feel. The SPACE + DATA + SHIFT = CHANGE equation simplifies the process.

Gather your information (DATA), give yourself room inside your head and with your actions for it to have a positive effect (SPACE), and you will eventually

SHIFT and get the CHANGE you long to experience. Sustain that CHANGE long enough and you will have new, automatic habits.

Remember...
SPACE + DATA + SHIFT = CHANGE

OBSERVE

Observation of others will give you vital information and place you in a powerful position of knowledge. Observing others will also let you see what is and what is not working for them. Ask others how they broke a bad habit. If they gave it up "cold turkey," what did they do in place of the bad habit? Could it be that they used their own version of FIVE SECOND LIGHTSWITCH when they gave up their habit?

Bo Lozoff wrote a book about the spiritual path entitled "Deep and Simple." Here is one passage that might be helpful in the process of embracing your own magnificence:

DEEP AND SIMPLE

You may say, "I don't know what to believe in, I don't even know what you mean by my 'deepest values'." But if you don't know you've got a thousand dollars in your wallet, it doesn't mean you're broke. It just means you must learn to look though your wallet more thoroughly. Your heart is a wallet which holds deep values and vast riches; it isn't empty, I assure you. You may simply not have looked through it for a while. That's one important aspect of personal spiritual practice.

Bo Lozoff
"Deep and Simple," Page 81

CONSIDER THIS...

FIVE SECOND LIGHTSWITCH
is a powerful tool for diverting
the neurological traffic
reinforcing a bad habit.

FIVE SECOND LIGHTSWITCH
will empower you to consider
the reasons you decided
to give up the habit
in the first place.

FIVE SECOND LIGHTSWITCH
will allow you to create NEW
thought, new behaviors
and new habits.

FIVE SECOND LIGHTSWITCH
In Action

THE GUARD

Let's say there is one particular guard who really has it out for you. We will call him Hector. Hector never liked you and you are not quite certain what you may have done to get him so focused on making your life miserable.

Hector is having a particularly bad day. It seems that everyone in the yard is suffering from a severe case of raw nerves. Spirits are low.

The newly arrived warden seems to be wielding his authority in some interesting ways, undoubtedly rattling Hector and the other guards with new task lists and requirements.

It is movement time for your area and you are headed to your job in the kitchen. Hector yells across the yard for you to come over to him. Knowing that you can't be late for work, you are irritated and hope Hector isn't going to pull anything stupid because you are just about ready to tell him where he can shove it. When he tells you to go to A Unit to deliver a message you can't help but respond, "What's your radio for?"

Instantly you know that there is more in store from Hector and you regret mouthing off to him. FIVE SECOND LIGHTSWITCH empowers you to handle Hector and people *like Hector far more effectively. Your <u>reaction</u> to the "Hectors" of the world speaks everything about who you are.*

The world knows about people like Hector. They see this type of person moving through life in their self-consumed, miserable manner. What they do not know is how you react to the "Hectors" of the world. How you react says everything about you and nothing about Hector.

FIVE SECOND LIGHTSWITCH IN ACTION

1) THOUGHTS ENTER - The desire to haul off and plant a firm fist into Hector's blabbering mouth is pretty strong right now. He has pushed you beyond an acceptable limit and you have just got to set this guy straight.

2) PERMISSION GRANTED - Instead of being upset that you are having these thoughts, you let your mind notice this urge. In fact, think about what is happening with your thoughts for a full five seconds. You can even entertain the outcome if you were to act on your urge.

Let the THOUGHT (not the action) exist for FIVE FULL SECONDS.

There was a time when acting on these kinds of thoughts was something you just automatically did without thinking. Notice that, too.

For five full seconds you can just think about what you are thinking about. Isn't it interesting how automatic your reaction to Hector became? It is almost as if Hector knew which buttons to push. He pushed them and you reacted like a puppet.

3) THOUGHT SWAP - Now you will swap the thought for something more powerful. On the sixth second, you take over the wheel of the car and head in a different direction.

Think to yourself, "What is it going to take for me to get myself back on my job and away from this heated situation?" or "I want peace more than I want to spend a week in the hole. What can I do to make peace right now?" or "This is an old pattern that never worked for me. No matter if I'm right or wrong, it is time to do things differently."

4) REPEAT REPEAT REPEAT - You can think and rethink new ways of responding while Hector's temperature begins to boil.

Take a subtle step back to get a bit more physical distance between you and Hector. Take a deep breath using BELLY BREATHING and take control of the wheel of the car and do what you need to do to steer yourself to safety.

"Weed? – Wait – "Workout?"

In this case, your RESULTS are more important than what you believe is RIGHT. Nothing that you say is going to change the fact that Hector thinks he is right. There is no room for discussion.

Hector may write you up for being disrespectful and not following an order. He will be correct and you will spend some dark days thinking about how much you hate him, how right you were, and how you can't wait to see him on the street one day.

Instead, flip a light switch in your mind. Realize old ways of behaving are no longer out of your control. You have the power to send the neurological river anywhere that <u>you</u> choose to send it.

As corny as it sounds on paper, you may choose to say to Hector, "It was out of line for me to say that. I didn't mean to pop off. For some reason things seem tense on the yard for me today."

Or you can stand neutral and say nothing, choosing to wait for a repeat of the order that will help you decide the quickest plan to get back to work.

WHY IT WORKS

FIVE SECOND LIGHTSWITCH works and becomes easier over time. FIVE SECOND LIGHTSWITCH allows you to "go with the flow" and also change its direction.

Remember, it is easier to move traffic to the left or right than to try to stop a long line of fast moving cars head on.

Your automatic responses are like rivers of information flowing through your body. Don't spend a lot amount of time thinking about them when you can take action to divert the flow of information and achieve more positive reactions.

Think of it like a river. It's easier to divert water running down a river than it is to stop the river flow altogether.

FIVE SECOND LIGHTSWITCH works because it puts you in the position of acknowledging the bad habit or the automatic thought. It diverts your attention toward the desired response. In this way, you acknowledge that the water is flowing and you subtly divert it to a new direction.

It is easier to divert running water than to stop it. If a car is headed in the wrong direction, rather than automatically jerking the wheel to steer it, try gently guiding it back to one that you intend.

You can let the moods, words, actions and reactions of others pull you off course. Or you can make the decision to nudge yourself back on course by using the tools that you have gathered thus far: BOSS OF YOUR BRAIN, BELLY BREATHING, FIVE SECOND LIGHTSWITCH. Pull these tools out of your toolbox whenever they are needed.

It is inevitable that you will change. You will continue to change throughout your life. As you widen your perspective, you will begin to notice how others operate and why they operate in the manner that they do. Through your awareness, you will start to notice how you can stealthy avoid 99 percent of confrontations and obstacles.

Begin to observe. Through observation, you will learn from the mistakes and accomplishments of others.

Words from a brother...

The first thing you understand when you are on the inside is the prison staff. Most of them don't give a damn about you. It's hard to find the ones that do. But this is where you have to take advantage of the programs and absorb the game that is given.

Keep this game tight on a daily basis. Under the prison settings it's a negative thing anyway. But you can make it positive if you go within yourself.

Your gunna get words from your family members cuz they are going to try do discourage you because they have only seen you one way. It is just like they are waiting in the cut for me to fail so they can say, "I told you so."

But if I focus on that, instead of focusing on what is good, I will fail.

So, you do this for yourself and nobody else.

It's possible, man. It's possible.

OBSERVE OTHERS...

Take a few moments today to speak less. Observing the habits of others is usually easier if you keep your own thoughts silent.

You can begin to witness their automatic reactions and automatic behavior.

You might observe them abdicating their ability to create the kind of life that they want. Then you will see how powerless they truly have become. You will see that for all their posturing and tough-guy talk, they are really at the mercy of situations and others around them.

How would you use THE FIVE SECOND LIGHTSWITCH if you were suffering from old patterns of behavior of others that continues day after day?

What new habit would you create as a replacement?

Also, observe yourself...

When could you begin to use the FIVE SECOND LIGHTSWITCH as a tool to get you back in the driver's seat of your life?

Try the FIVE SECOND LIGHTSWITCH in one specific area of your life. Test it out long enough to let it work.

Maybe you can pick one person and begin to build an alternate response pattern to their predictable communication.

By the way, the FIVE SECOND LIGHTSWITCH helps enormously with two of the most powerful automatic habits that people give up their power — drug addiction and compulsive thoughts.

CHAPTER SEVEN

WHAT IF?

Words from a brother...
Now What If?
What if I was born with a silver spoon in my mouth?
Would I be happy? What if I never went to prison? Would
I still feel like I am feeling right now?
The important "What If?" is what if you are so beat
down and needed a way out.
What if you picked this book up and really used it?
What would your life be like? If you were willing, what
would life be like?
Like I said before, if you won the lotto would life get
better? Or would it get worse because the ego will get bigger?
So I'm asking and recommending, is that you put
yourself in a position to say "What If?" I fill my mind with
rightness? Would I be this way now? Today?
I ask myself that same question. But we have one
thing... we all have the capability of being willing.
What If man! What If?

Your intention becomes your reality

By now you might be seeing small and subtle differences in your life if you are reading this book with the sincere intent of creating a powerful life for yourself.

Your experiences with others might be different. You might see new opportunities or obstacles more clearly. You might simply be irritated that there are a bunch of people around you who are not in control of their thinking or behaving.

If things are subtly changing, either negatively or positively, then you are benefiting from:

The SPACE + DATA + SHIFT = CHANGE equation

- SPACE, is room in your thinking that helps you to think and consider options for your life. If this is the case then . . .

- You may be benefiting from new DATA, or new information, and you are giving yourself. . .

- A SHIFT and you are primed for

- CHANGE, and for new behaviors and reactions to occur.

Know your tools. Practice the tools until they become second nature:

1) BOSS OF YOUR BRAIN
2) BELLY BREATHING and
3) FIVE SECOND LIGHTSWITCH

Along the path of your journey, you may have modified or altered some of the steps to fit your own unique interpretation or style. Great. Make them yours. Put your unique stamp on the way you run your personal thought process.

The tools are not designed to fit every individual in the same way. They are flexible generalities that can be adjusted to fit your own interpretation or success strategies.

If these tools work exactly as described…that's great. It's also fine if they need a little modification to fit your own personal needs. The point is that you may fine-tune the tools and make them yours.

These body tools permit new DATA (new information delivered in a new way), and allow you the SPACE (the internal environment), to "rewire" your brain for the SHIFT leading to CHANGE.

As you begin to put these tools into practice, you will likely realize that you can control these tools in addition to controlling your thoughts.

The WHAT IF? tool for your toolbox of change is more concept related. Rather than a tangible or physiological process, WHAT IF? will tap into your unlimited potential for imagination and creativity.

This tool gives you permission to imagine possibilities, consider options, and provide a direction of which you can steer your intentions.

The next tool is WHAT IF?

WHAT IF? is important for anyone who feels stuck, trapped, or cornered in a way that restricts them from being the very best they can be.

WHAT IF? can help a good athlete become a better one. WHAT IF? can help an addict see avenues of hope. WHAT IF? can help an inmate experiment with new ways of thinking and reacting in the world.

WHAT IF? actually moves you into your ability to creatively imagine alternatives.

WHAT IF? challenges you to look beyond the obvious and toward possibilities.

There is a tendency to believe that the environment or the people in your life exert control over your feelings, thoughts or reactions.

In truth, no one has control over your thoughts. No person, no event, no situation, no punishment, no mistake, no phone call or judge's gavel has control over your thoughts. And, no person, no event, no situation, no punishment, no mistake, no phone call or judge's gavel has control over your reactions to anything in your life.

Remember Bo Lozoff's analogy that incarceration is as if the individual has been tossed off society's train, tumbling down the bank and onto the barren soil of a desert? Remember, too, that he suggests society, as we know it, might be headed for a train wreck from which you have been spared.

The People of GOGI

Freedom on the inside.

There are unlimited ways to experience each event. Here is an example of how people perceive their surroundings differently.

<u>200 Different Versions of the Truth</u>

There may be a couple hundred individuals in a movie theater sitting in similar chairs and eating similar junk food. They will watch the same big screen for 90 minutes. The same big images flash before them.

Yet, the movie experience is different and unique to each of the 200 individuals — and none is identical.

Check this out next time you watch a movie with a group of people. There will be just as many different observations as there are sets of eyes when the movie is finished.

As they leave the theater, 200 different experiences have occurred. There may be consensus of "that was good" or "that was a waste of time," but the individual experience is quite.... Individual.

After enough individuals concur that a movie experience falls into the "good" category, then word of mouth travels and Hollywood marketing efforts are heightened and the movie may earn millions upon millions of dollars.

Still, even when there is a general consensus of good or bad, each individual will have their own separate experience.

What if our society was truly under siege and the only safe place was inside a State or Federal prison? Would your experience behind the wall be different? Would you live every day in gratitude for being spared from the train wreck?

The prison of higher education

After high school graduation, many of the U.S. youth attend college or universities rather than starting work in a fulltime career.

The reasons for attending additional schooling are different. Every semester there are different types of adults who pay application fees and pack for school.

Some do not have any idea what career or job to pursue. Enrolling in additional classes buys them time to figure things out. Maybe their parents support a specific goal or career. Parents might "force" their child to attend college to avoid living at home, watching too many video games or eating fast food.

There are many reasons that college campuses fill up with young adults. And the students need to jump through a lot of hoops before they can graduate. Some college campuses are isolated from a main city center. Those students might feel trapped.

There is a dress code at many of these institutions of higher learning. Students must attend a predetermined set of classes that are offered at predetermined days and times. They must earn a specific number of credits. They sneak out to drink a beer or have a smoke. They eat terrible food at predetermined and rigidly set hours in a mess hall. The canned food dished out onto plastic bowls and placed on worn trays is unhealthy and unappetizing. They have a tiny cot on which they sleep. The showers are often large rooms with wet floors seething with fungus.

Many of the students have entry-level, minimum wage jobs in addition to the academic requirement. Most of them are broke, tired, anxious, and look forward to graduation. Many have school loans at the end of their sentence. Loan payments might span over 30 years.

Basically, the entire student body is held captive by an unbending administration that holds a thick rulebook over their heads. They essentially become sentenced to 4 years of academic imprisonment when they choose higher education.

How would you feel about incarceration if you believed that it was a laboratory in which you could experiment with personal change goals?

How would you feel about incarceration if the only safe place was behind the wall? Undoubtedly, your spirits would lift and your energy would increase.

What if society had "met the train wreck" and the only survivors were prisoners?" Behind the walls, incarcerated individuals would start making plans to rebuild the barren world.

WHAT IF?

What if there was a crystal ball that revealed that you would meet an untimely death by means of a city bus? But luckily, you were incarcerated instead.

You were spared from death and given an opportunity to live on earth for many more years. It's true that you are behind a wall. But isn't it better to be alive? Try to appreciate simple pleasures like a friendly smile or a completion of a task.

What if reality is just an illusion? Being behind a wall still allows you the right for a happier life than many of the "free" people — a life of integrity and personal empowerment.

The People of GOGI

Coach Taylor with GOGI Supporter Troy Byer.

Coach Mia and Graduate Wally at the GOGI office.

Your REAL Job

What if your "job" on the inside is to educate and empower others through your examples? You will return to society so fortified, and so solid that nothing and no one can shake you.

What if you are a force for good just waiting to happen? WHAT IF?

This is what I see each and every time I enter a facility. I see men and women who are better at educating at-risk and incarcerated individuals than those who get paid to educate them.

I see men and women who could easily be trained to be Social Workers, Psychologists, teachers, Coaches, and leaders. They could be teaching and guiding other people to stop making the same mistakes.

I see hugely influential individuals sitting in the yard, bored beyond all reasonable levels of boredom. They seem to be uninspired and drained of creativity. I think of the promise that their experiences hold. I think of the good that they can and should do.

What if their "job," their "task," their "mission" and their "rehabilitation requirements" was to keep 3 individuals from heading down the slippery slope?

What if we used our weaknesses and made them our finest strengths?

WHAT IF?

Coach Taylor

How we choose to see something is the determining factor in our experiences.

Perception is everything.   This is what makes WHAT IF? so powerful.

How many arrests can be avoided if WHAT IF? is utilized?
WHAT IF? this cop is just having a bad day?
WHAT IF? I can avoid arrest and continue on my way?

Safe On The Inside

One boy I "coached" spent most of his life in long or short-term "visits" to almost every Juvenile Justice Department facility in Los Angeles.

The other day his worried mother called me because he was arrested, again. She wanted my advice. Her son was involved in a car accident when he had been driving drunk. He now had a "strike two" with the California justice department. He is only nineteen.

A strange part of me – in fact, nearly all of me – was very grateful that he was locked up. He had been spinning out of control for months. It was only a matter of time before I got a call that he had met the wrong side of a bullet.

While he sits in County awaiting the first in a long series of court sessions, he is undoubtedly discouraged and probably pissed off. He probably feels rage and blames everyone but himself.

Me? I am grateful. I am happy that he is locked up. No one was killed. No guns were fired. And, he is safe – from himself.

WHAT IF? behind bars for a while is the only way to keep him alive?

WHAT IF? your incarceration is really an opportunity for you? Could it permit you to live a long and productive life?

Coach Taylor

R. D. Laing is a psychologist who has a good ability of looking at the problems of his clients. He empowers the client to see beyond their self-imposed limitations.

Here is a quote from R. D. Laing that you may find helpful. You, too, can stretch and move beyond your present limited perception of truth and reality.

Simply Failing to Notice

The range of what we think and do is limited by what we fail to notice and because WE FAIL TO NOTICE THAT WE FAIL TO NOTICE there is little we can do to change until we notice how failing to notice shapes our thoughts and deeds.

R.D. Laing
Psychologist

What you choose to notice and do in your life speaks volumes of the individual that you choose to be.

An inmate made the following assessment a few months ago during one large GOGI class. He said that he was not able to be "free." It was only after he was locked up that he found internal freedom.

While some guys humbly nodded with understanding, other class members scoffed at his statement.

They remarked that there nothing good could that comes from being locked behind bars.

And, how could anything good happen?

Think about it! Being physically free does not guarantee freedom.

After all, their families need food, bills paid, and work that needs to be done.

As a matter of fact, the scoffing individuals had legitimate reasons to hold onto their perceptions.

However, they were not free from the confines of their perception.

It does not take freedom to be free.

And being physically "free" does not guarantee freedom.

The Difference Between Prison and Work
An anonymous e-mail

In Prison: You spend the majority of your time in a 10x10 cell.
At Work: You spend the majority of your time in an 8x8 cubicle.

In Prison: You get 3 meals a day.
At Work: You get 1 break a day and have to pay for it.

In Prison: You get time off for good behavior.
At Work: You get more work for good behavior.

In Prison: The guard locks and unlocks the doors for you.
At Work: You must often carry a security card and open all the
           doors yourself.

In Prison: You can watch TV and play games.
At Work: You get sacked for the above.

In Prison: You get your own toilet.
At Work: You share a toilet with co-workers and strangers.

In Prison: They allow your friends and family to visit.
At Work: You aren't even supposed to speak to your family.

In Prison: All expenses are paid by the taxpayer with no work
           required.
At Work: You get to pay all your expenses to work and they
           deduct taxes from your salary to pay for prisoners.

In Prison: You spend most of your time behind bars wanting to
           get out.
At Work: You spend most of your time wanting to get out and
           go inside bars.

In Prison: You deal with wardens.
At Work: They are called managers.

THE TOOL OF "WHAT IF?" will:

- Help you see previously overlooked perspectives and possibilities. You will look at every challenge, every event, every opinion, every reaction, and every action in a different way.

- Help you think new thoughts about new possibilities. You will be empowered with data accumulated through your willingness to consider options.

- Help you take actions based on the new thoughts and possibilities. You will see how others approach similar situations. You will be able to build competencies through the examples of others.

- Help you break old habits, and replace them with ones that are more successful. You will be willing to develop new neurological pathways leading to new habits.

THE TRUTH IS. . .

WHAT IF? allows you to see things in a new way. You will be empowered to see options and opportunities that others fail to see.

WHAT IF? places you in an immediate position of self empowerment because you will see the many options that you really have — even in the most difficult situations.

WHAT IF? helps you make SMARTER, STRONGER decisions because you will see other points of view and other options.

HOW WHAT IF? WORKS

WHAT IF? is the practice of looking at any situation from an different seat in the theater of life.

Remember the 200 individuals in the movie theater? The person in each seat generates a slightly different perception. There are alternate realities and other available options.

WHAT IF? is a question that you ask yourself continually.

Coach Taylor outside a prison in Romania.

Willingness to let go of your deep-rooted opinions permits the expansion of ideas and awareness.

As you assume WHAT IF? your brain is open to new neurological pathways. These are potential truths from which you can create thought and action.

You shift towards a new reality that has accessible options. With What IF? you are able to pull your thoughts away from old habits or patterns.

ADDED BENEFITS OF WHAT IF?

Consider the WHAT IF? option in every situation. There is an additional benefit to asking yourself "WHAT IF?" Anger will not come as quickly with you newfound flexibility. You are likely to get along better with others and have improved relationships. .

WHY WHAT IF? WORKS…

Behavior is often based on the reactions of others. Your reactions are no longer automatic when you realize that you have options. You are inclined to think before you react if you have choices.

There may be a huge difference in the outcome of events by taking a pause before actions. Asking WHAT IF? generates a "pause" that permits you to consider options.

To a large extent, you can model behaviors until they become habits. Ask yourself, "WHAT IF? I was a calm person, how would I breathe?" "WHAT IF? I was lucky, how would I speak?' "WHAT IF I was very successful, how would I carry myself?"

PUTTING WHAT IF? INTO PRACTICE

You can control your actions if you can control your thoughts. An easy tool for controlling thoughts is to think about how another person might perceive the same situation.

Straight A Students

I work with a group of 5th grade boys attending a Watts, California, area elementary school. The GOGI team of coaches and I teach the GETTING OUT BY GOING IN concepts for self-empowerment and solid decision-making skills.

Several boys at the school were labeled as having behavioral problems. Both the teachers and parents gave quick approval for the boys to spend time a "behavioral coach."

I used the WHAT IF? question one day when the group of rowdy 5th graders was particularly uncooperative. I asked "WHAT IF? you were all 'A-students' How would you be behaving right now?"

They quickly sat up straight, clasped their hands and became extraordinarily quiet.

I asked them "So, you would choose to sit straight and at attention if you were all straight A-students?"

They nodded in reply.

"I bet it feels pretty cool to be A-students?" I asked.

They all smiled.

The boys made a choice to change their behavior.

The new behavior was contrary to the labels that were given to them throughout the school system.

They were able to test out new ways of being and behaving when presented with "WHAT IF?"

Coach Taylor

As simple as it seems, the WHAT IF? is likely to transform your actions and reactions in just about every situation. Here are the simple steps to the WHAT IF?

STEP 1) INCOMING INFORMATION - Incoming information can be processed in many different ways.

Every piece of information is automatically assigned a meaning from habit. How the information is processed is determined by our attitude, outlook and expectations.

For example, information is processed in unconstructive and unproductive ways if your attitude is negative. As a result, your behavior and reactions are adversely affected.

On the other hand, reactions and behavior will be constructive and confident if the information is processed in a positive manner.

The WHAT IF? question allows you to maintain control of your thoughts and how you process information. Control of your thoughts will help you take control of your behavior.

What happens when you begin to use the WHAT IF? question? You will experience the incoming information in a new way before you generate a response.

STEP 2) BELLY BREATHING – Breathe the way you were born to breathe - with the entire body involved. This way of breathing buys you time for paying attention to how you respond to events and situations. It also sends oxygen to your brain that permits you to think smartly. When you breathe properly, you can relax more. You make better decisions when you are relaxed.

STEP 3) WHAT IF? – If the BOSS OF YOUR BRAIN doesn't get you over an obstacle — or the FIVE SECOND LIGHTSWITCH doesn't quite work — you can start to ask some WHAT IF? questions.

Ask yourself, "If I was headed towards the airport for a Hawaiian vacation with $1,000, how would I react? What would I really care about?"

Or… "Five years from now, will I still be upset about someone else's reactions?

Or… "How would I handle this situation if I was not reliant upon this individual?"

It is powerful to ask WHAT IF? questions. Consider different ways to react to situations. WHAT IF? lets the incident stand on its own by taking all the variables out of the equation.

Do not let feelings or emotions become attached to incidents that you experience. Move on to the next step of the WHAT IF? process if they cloud your judgment.

STEP 4) ANOTHER "WHAT IF" - Let's say that the situation is so distressing that there is no way to pull away from your attachments and change a particular meaning.

Ask yourself a dozen WHAT IF? questions, if you need to. Consider as many options as you can. Give some thought to as many different perspectives as you can.

A real common WHAT IF? is "What would Jesus do?" You can substitute Jesus for just about anyone you admire or respect. Another way to capture the "WHAT IF" mentality is to imagine how someone else might respond.

Ask yourself, "If this happened to. . .Mother Teresa. . . Michael Jordan. . . your mentor. . . Your meditation teacher.... ANYONE ELSE. . . How would they handle it?" Ask yourself how they would respond, how they would reply, how they might breathe, or how they would think. You will actually feel a different response when you mimic, imitate, or even FAKE someone else's response.

FAKE IT UNTIL YOU MAKE IT HAPPEN...

You may discover that there is an immense value in "faking it until you make it" as you learn new ways of responding to circumstances.

New neurological pathways form new responses when you fake alternative reactions for 21 days. These pathways essentially reinforce new habits.

Faking is the perfect way to create new neural possibilities and permits your body to respond in a desirable way. It allows you to take charge of your body and become the BOSS OF YOUR BRAIN.

The WHAT IF? questions are really a way for you to master the BOSS OF YOUR BRAIN tool.

You will control your reality through empowering new perceptions.

THINK ABOUT IT

With a lack of information in events or circumstances, you might may make poor decisions or conclusions. You are more empowered to lead than blindly follow if you are aware of all sides of a story or situation.

Consider an instance when you reacted hastily to information before you obtained additional information. Did you understand the perspective better when you were able to listen to another's point of view?

Is it possible that the way you first react to a situation is not necessarily the best response?

Is it possible that you might respond differently with supplementary data obtained from asking WHAT IF? questions?

Take a moment to reflect on some of your past reactions. Think about the different situations.

How do you think that your Pastor, the Pope, God, grandmother, a child, Martin Luther King, or ANYONE ELSE would react to the same situation?

What is happening in your life right now? Is the habit of being angry, judgmental, critical, or self-critical serving you in any way?

Does this negative habit keep you stuck? Does it have a purpose?

Ask yourself some WHAT IF? questions and consider some new possibilities.

WHAT IF? you were considered to be the calmest individual on the yard?

WHAT IF? people asked you how you are able to stay calm in the face of chaos?

WHAT IF? you were the kind of individual who could see many different perspectives simultaneously?

Words from a brother...

When you have learned to use this information, these tools, you got to give it away. Because you will be watched by everybody, probation officers, neighbors, friends, anyone who knows you prior to your getting out by going in. Giving it away strengthens you.

Information is very important. It is also matters how you use the information. Don't worry about tomorrow, or two weeks from tomorrow. Live in the now. Think about now, share the information now. What you are going to think and do right now?

WATCH OTHERS

Observing others gives you vital information and places you in a powerful position of understanding.

Observe someone who is angry. Are they giving themselves enough time to consider other ways of reacting? Are they reacting out of habit? Are they accomplishing their objective with anger? What does their limited perspective tell you about them?

Your observation of others is a powerful tool.

You will know more about how they operate. You can assess what behaviors are similar to ones that you want to release in favor of finding freedom.

Observe others - truly observe others – from a compassionate stance.

You will be further empowered to be the boss of your brain. You will not let habits or old ways of thinking and behaving "run your program" when you are the boss of your brain.

There is no law that limits your internal growth. There is no law that regulates how you respond to things.

The People of GOGI

GOGI Volunteer Coach Helen, Coach DJ, Coach Taylor and GOGI Volunteer Coach Debbie at a recent GOGI graduation. During the weekly classes, all participants learned BOSS OF YOUR BRAIN and other GOGI techniques.

CONSIDER THIS...

WHAT IF?

*is one of the most
powerful tools for
opening up the possibilities
of new responses and reactions.*

WHAT IF? *will permit you
to see the other person's point
of view and you are more likely
to start effective communication
when you understand
their motivation.*

> # WHAT IF?
> ## In Action

MIKE GETS FIRED

It took Mike months to land a job. The only problem is that he does not have respect his supervisor. The supervisor shows up late or hung-over, and berates most of the employees, especially Mike. In fact, Mike is the only one who got "written up" for infractions that everyone else gets away with.

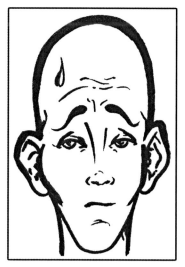

When Mike showed up for work after the long weekend, and learned that his boss had fired him. His supervisor blamed him for everyone else's mistakes and no one defended Mike.

Mike was not in a position to be unemployed and finding a job is never an easy task with an ex-felon stamp on your forehead. He did not have any savings and the bills were stacked high. The more he thought about how unfair the situation was, the angrier he got.

To let the questions of WHAT IF? work for him, Mike needed to take control of his thoughts.

First, he did BELLY BREATHING to get his body to relax. He knew he was more intelligent when his body was relaxed.

Then… **WHAT IF? IN ACTION**

1) INCOMING INFORMATION - Mike got the news that he was fired. Out of habit, he automatically got mad at the supervisor. He wanted to tell his side of the story. Being fired meant that he was taking the fall for his supervisor's dishonesty and inability to do a good job. Mike got angry. Getting angry was not Mike's most intelligent state of mind. He needs a neurological wedge. Otherwise, he will travel down that same worn road that does him more harm than good.

2) BREATHE - Doing BELLY BREATHING gave Mike a little more time to take control of his thoughts and actions. Breathing helped him process information intelligently. Mike began to breathe and let his entire body relax. He considers some of his options: BOSS OF YOUR BRAIN and FIVE SECOND LIGHTSWITCH are tools he can use. In this case, however, he decides WHAT IF? will work to empower him and get him on the path that he has set for himself.

3) WHAT IF? - Once Mike had taken a breath, he asked himself, "If I had a pocket full of cash and I was headed to the airport, how would I react? What would I really care about?" With a little emotional distance, Mike realized that he would eventually get another job. He will be relieved that he will no longer work for his unsupportive supervisor.

4) ANOTHER WHAT IF? - Let's say that the situation is very disturbing. Not even the idea of cash or an airline ticket helps Mike see things differently. Mike then looks fast-forward into his life.

Thinking to himself, "I know that I am going to get work somewhere else. WHAT IF? I had the new job right now? How would I feel? How someone else would handle getting fired? What are other ways for me to handle situation?"

Mike continues to consider possibilities. What if this happened to ...Martin Luther King....Jesus....The Buddha ...ANYONE ELSE.... How would they handle the situation?" He asks himself, "How would God react? Coach Taylor? Bo Lozoff? Coach DJ? Homer Simpson?"

The answer will be clear if Mike asks this question while breathing fully. This job is just a job. He had jobs in the past and he will have jobs in the future. Future jobs are likely to be more supportive of his talents and skills. Being out of a job is inconvenient because of financial challenges. He will immediately look for a job that better fits his skills.

When Mike chooses to mimic, imitate, and even FAKE how someone else might respond he feels very differently about the situation. He is more objective and less angry.

It will be tough to get a good job in such short notice. Yet, he realizes that he did not care for this job much and that he has been in worse situations.

WHY IT WORKS

The WHAT IF? technique works because it gives you the power over your habits and automatic responses.
When you see powerful and positive reactions of others, you can adopt them for yourself.

OBSERVE OTHERS...

This week your challenge is to notice how people react. Are they automatically reacting or are they considering options before they respond?
Do they breathe before reacting or is the reaction rapid and without much thought?

Also, observe yourself...

What happens when you practice the WHAT IF? question in your daily routine? Under what situations is it difficult? When is it easy to consider options of acting and reacting?

The muscles of change develop over time. Keep at it, just like going to the gym for your body. Build your mental muscles in the same manner, over time.

Words from a brother...

What if ?

Right now. The peace you feel. If you could share that with the other 1,400 men on the yard, there would be peace on every prison yard. There would be no prison politics, no drama. Honestly ask yourself, because I have asked myself, the What If? question.

Speaking about prison politics, the first thing you learn is where you sit at in the chow hall. Blacks sit here, whites sit there, Hispanics sit there, and the Asians sit there, Native Americans sit over there.

Everything is segregated. Basically, when you go to a chow hall it reminds you of Sunday. You have black churches over there, white churches over there. Religious politics. There is no peace in segregation. There is only peace in unity.

Now, let me touch on the yard politics. One small incident can cause a full-scale riot. Honestly speaking, when I was on yard and I knew it was jump off, the only thought was "would I catch a new case?"

So when its time to suit up I think about everything good under my circumstances. Going on visits. Working at Unicore, watching TV, lifting weights. The basic privileges we have on the yard. I think, "I am going to get transferred to another state. I am going to be in special housing unit for some months?" I know I am not the only one who ever felt like that.

My white partners be talking about the same thing. My Asian partners be talking about the same thing. My Mexican partners be talking about the same thing.

Without these tools, these techniques and this education, the only avenue we could take was to ride it out. Attend these classes, these programs. When you see a flyer in the unit education or psychology and it has GOGI on it, go to it, attend it and you won't have the What If? in regret.

Influence the homies, especially them youngsters, in a positive light. You will become peaceful, the yard becomes peaceful, and the prison is no longer a prison but a place of re-construction of our mind, body and soul. Peace.

The People of GOGI

Principal Edward Brownlee (far right) is pictured with the students of GOGI's class at Hillcrest High School in Inglewood, California. The students took a tour of Pepperdine University as part of an introduction into life's possibilities with a High School degree. WHAT IF?

GOGI Supporter & friend, Sita Lozoff

Sunlight shines through one of Sita Lozoff's stained glass windows.

Sita Lozoff and Coach Taylor.

Sita Lozoff's hobby is making stained glass windows. This one of Neem Karoli (above) is one of her favorties.

TOOLS FOR THE SPIRIT

Tom Kratochvil, Ph.D., MFT, FSICPP, DAPA
Licensed Marriage and Family Therapist

_____

December, 2006

To Whom It May Concern:

This letter introduces you to the California non-profit organization *GETTING OUT BY GOING IN* (GOGI) and the *SIGN UP FOR SUCCESS!* initiative for at-risk adults and youth. It is designed to help in the fight against recidivism in our justice system.

As a southern California probation officer for over 19 years and a Marriage and Family Therapist, I have come to work with literally hundreds of law breakers. Research in the field of behavior problems has shown that the application of cognitive psychology techniques has been useful in working toward the prevention of criminal behavior, plus the building of self-esteem and positive image. The GOGI *SIGN UP FOR SUCCESS!* model offers a simple, understandable, and easy way for those at criminal risk to find self-worth and awareness and better communicate not only with others, but within themselves. All this based on cognitive psychology.

Positive self-talk, the internal thinking we all do, is one of the most vital communications there is. According to some experts, it comprises up to 90% of all our communication. It only stands to reason that having a bright, positive, and confident edge to life is a step in the right direction. But don't think that GOGI is just a one-time motivational shot in the arm! It is a series of actual easy and fun-to-learn tools that plant the seeds for personal motivation and self-worth and help to make them grow within the individual.

Please carefully and intuitively read the GOGI materials presented. While there is no panacea or "one size fits all" program for working with criminally at-risk people, I believe you will agree that the content and simplicity of the SIGN UP FOR SUCCESS! program is right on the mark for helping those at-risk make better lives for themselves in the years to come.

Thank you,

Tom Kratochvil, Ph.D.

Tom Kratochvil, Ph.D., MFT

CHAPTER EIGHT
POSITIVE TWA
POSITIVE THOUGHTS, WORDS, ACTIONS

A recent scientific study conducted by the University of Michigan explored "Positive Attitude," as it relates to human growth and success. They invested a great deal of time and resources and came up with an obvious result.

They found a correlation, or a link, between having a positive attitude and experiencing positive outcomes.

It may seem common sense, but very few of us actually focus on the positive things in our life. However, most people agree that looking at the "brighter side" of life is important.

Positive Thoughts, Words and Actions offer positive results, even if it is only in your positive perception or positive experience of negative stimuli.

With positive relationships, you are more pleasant when positive attributes are emphasized — even if the other person never changes!

Think about it. How much of your thinking, vocabulary and actions are negative? Are they negative because your situation is negative?

Are you reacting negatively and justifying it by the situation? Is the other person wrong? "They" did it?

Are you negative because the world needs to be a supportive place for you to be positive? Do things need to be positive around you in order for you to be positive as well?

Do you really want to give up control and live in reaction to your environment?

Think about the words you use daily. Are they "negative," "positive" or "neutral?" You might be surprised how many words might fall in the negative category.

Some individuals have negative viewpoints. Their spouse has 101 faults that "make" them unhappy.

Their situation has a million and one things that keep them from being internally happy.

Some individuals tend to blame their outlook on situations...their partner...their job...the system...anyone but themselves.

"I'd be happy if I was home," or "I'd be happy if I had money," or "I'd be happy if I had a good paying job."

A fundamental truth:

1) **POSITIVE THOUGHTS** - help you start the pathway toward positive living.

2) **POSITIVE WORDS** - your word choice leads to the actions you choose. Your word choice determines your positive or negative outcome.

3) **POSITIVE ACTIONS** - your actions are a result of your thoughts and your words. Your actions broadcast who you are to the world and what you are thinking.

Where do we start?

Everyone has unique positive traits. What are yours? Are you patient? Enthusiastic? Loyal? Peaceful?

Ask someone close to you for help in identifying positive traits. What are YOUR three best qualities? What are THEIR three best qualities?

Focus on three of your best qualities regularly. Your three best qualities will help you with your Thoughts, Words and Actions. POSITIVE TWA – Positive Thoughts, Words, Actions.

POSITIVE TWA allows you to use techniques proven by scientists and human behaviorists.

**Positive thoughts precede a
Positive life experience.**

Positive thoughts lead directly to positive words. It is difficult to be negative when you are thinking positive thoughts. The two are linked. Positive words lead to positive actions. Positive actions broadcast who you are to the world.

Try this…

When you have a negative thought, you can use the tools you have learned in this book. Try the Five Second Lightswitch and swap the thought with a positive thought. Give the thought five seconds and then swap it out with a positive one. "Yeah, it really sucks I have to go into work an hour earlier every day. That really cuts into my meditation time. I like meditating and we don't do anything the first hour, anyway," is how the thought pattern might go.

After five seconds of entertaining how terrible things are, swap it out with something like, "I am grateful and I like my job, I will actually get more done, it is likely that I will get off early, and no one is around that early so it will be peaceful. I can make this into a good thing for myself."

Make certain that you are headed toward a more positive experience for every negative thought. "Another mail call and there's nothing for me. No one cares," might be the reaction to an empty mailbag. Get three positive thoughts into your head as quickly as possible. "OK, so I received no letters. I guess I am not writing enough letters to the right people. But, I am sleeping better than before, I enjoyed the baseball game, my team won basketball last night." Any three positive thoughts will turn the tide toward positive words and positive actions. By doing so, you are likely to be more successful, healthier, and have better relationships. You will be happier when you get in the habit of replacing negative thoughts with a surplus of positive thoughts.

Use POSITIVE TWA towards creating a positive experience, regardless of what is going on around you. Positive THOUGHTS, WORDS and ACTIONS empower you to be the best that you can be. POSITIVE TWA – POSITIVE THOUGHTS, WORDS, AND ACTIONS.

POSITIVE TWA will help you:

- Remain positive about life regardless of the circumstance.

- Focus on your key positive traits and outnumber the negatives with positives.

- Create more opportunities to move forward in your life.

THE TRUTH IS. . .

*POSITIVE TWA allows
you to balance your
thoughts and words and actions
so that there are more positive
events than negative.*

*POSITIVE TWA reminds you to
consider your positive qualities and
trains your mind to look for
the positive in situations.*

*POSITIVE TWA
is based on the fact that positive
thoughts create the perceptual
experience of positive experiences.*

*(THOUGHTS, WORDS, ACTIONS)
TWA are three keys that allows
you to control your
thoughts, word, and actions.*

HOW DOES POSITIVE TWA?

POSITIVE TWA works on the premise that positive thoughts inspire positive words that create positive actions.

HERE'S WHY POSITIVE TWA WORKS…

Negative thoughts bathe your entire neurological system with negativity. Every cell of your body is receiving negative impulses much like being in a room with bad music blaring. Your body cannot escape the ramifications of negative (and positive) thought.

After you generate a thought, it leads to words. Unconstructive words filter throughout your body's neurology. The negative thoughts travel from your brain, through your body, out of your mouth and into the environment.

Negativity operates much like a radio signal and sends vibrations into the space around you. Basically, your ears hear those negative words when you talk trash about a person or a situation. The negativity permeates every cell of your body, bathing you with negative messages, even when you are talking about someone else!

Negativity filters deep into every cell of your body and experiences feelings from the words you generated.

For example, your entire body turns into one big bundle of negative energy when you are cussing at a guard who took you off the soccer field because he did not like how you wore your shirt. You, rather than he, pay the bigger price of your negative reaction. He may not like what you say and may write you up, but every cell of your body is in negative vibration.

Your thoughts are negative, your words are negative and your actions are negative. You lose.

Everyone experiences your negativity when you are upset and react in a negative way, but no one experiences it more profoundly than you do.

The good news is that research suggests that positive thoughts are more powerful than negative thoughts.

With positive thoughts, we can outweigh the impact of negativity easily. And, with enough practice, we can outweigh negativity effortlessly and automatically.

There are some individuals who barely see negativity. They focus beyond the negative into what is inherently positive about their life. For these individuals it does not take a place or a paycheck for internal freedom to occur.

POSITIVE TWA is a tool for you. Internal freedom is within your reach with POSITIVE TWA.

100 Good Things

I conducted my own mini-experiment one day at a youth prison. I gave each boy one of those $2.00 composition notebooks and a pencil. Their assignment was to write down 100 good things about themselves.

"I ain't got 100 good things about me, Coach," Jose responded.

"Do you brush your teeth?" I asked.

"Of course," he replied.

"Well, that is one really good thing about you, Jose. You brush your teeth. Write that down as the number one."

The lists were interesting and revealing. "I kiss good," "I like music," and "I like basketball" were often sandwiched between "my sister likes me" and "I am a good friend."

Eventually, each of the boys completed their list of 100 good qualities. Of that list of 100, they were to identify personal traits that they believed were their most important ones.

"I am a good friend," "I love my family" and "I am athletic," ranked among the most popular. "I am committed, loyal and dedicated" occasionally popped up in a few lists.

The boys realized that they had many good qualities. They were empowered to rely on these good qualities throughout their day.

The idea was to identify with something positive about yourself and use it when unproductive habits surface.

You can do the same.

Coach Taylor

With so many negatives around you, it is not easy to expect a positive outcome. It may seem very difficult to find anything positive in what appears to be a terribly bad situation. In truth, bad situations are saddening, maddening, discouraging and depressing.

Regardless of whether the situation changes or not, if we maintain positive TWA, positive THOUGHTS, WORDS and ACTIONS, our experience of the situation will be more tolerable.

Again, *even if our situation does not change, the experience of our situation will become more tolerable when we CHOOSE POSITIVE TWA.*

Where is the positive?

What could be good about getting fired? Divorced? Terminal illness? A loved one's death? There may be nothing positive, but how we choose to experience the negative is what is critical. Deep within ourselves, we can remain positive within a sea of negative. We find our own tiny morsel of goodness.

Sometimes the positive is not as hidden as we originally thought. What could be good about getting fired? Besides the "routine" of the daily workday, you might enter employment and discover mew opportunities. You might earn better pay. You might meet new people or find a new friend. You might get more enjoyment and less stress at the next job.

What could be good about getting a divorce? There is a chance that you will fall in love again and have an opportunity to build something better.

There is an opportunity to look within and take responsibility for yourself and not default to blaming your partner. You can't blame someone who is no longer a variable in your blame game.

What is good about the death of a loved one? You have fond memories from your experiences together. You learn to value life. You learn to seize each moment as if it were the last. You learn to love more deeply.

What is good about being locked up? Well…it depends on the direction of your focus. You have the opportunity to restructure your entire way of thinking, being, and reacting.

You can share learning with others. You can expand your perception of right and wrong. You can build a strategy for internal bliss.

You can meditate, work out, work, study new subjects, read and become very literate, crochet, write, and do lots of thinking about life's possibilities.

Internal freedom is within reach if you can distance yourself from the negative and fill every day with POSITIVE TWA while you are locked up.

Positive breeds positive

Those around you will have a positive experience when you verbalize positive words and every cell of your body reverberates with POSITIVE TWA. When you focus on POSITIVE TWA, it is highly probable that you will experience increasingly positive outcomes.

What we believe to be important today, including what really upsets us, are likely to have less importance tomorrow. Are they really worth being negative?

Children may lose their temper over not getting something they want, but within a few minutes, their attention is elsewhere. They move on to something else that is just as important.

An inmate may be stuck in the despair of their current situation. "Woe is me, I am locked up. My wife left me and my kid is in Juvi," can be moved closer to, "I can control my TWA. I cannot control my wife's departure. I cannot control my son's behavior. But I can be a positive force for everyone in my unit. I can be healthier and happier than I was yesterday. I can be positive and pray that my ex-wife and my son run into positive people like me."

Moving beyond a negative outlook leads to seeing positive aspects of a situation. Individuals who master TWA look and speak positive. They look toward change and have a far better chance of recovering from a relapse than their negative counterparts.

Positive individuals recover speedily because they do not wallow in what might be wrong with situations. They move towards the direction of possibilities. They push forward and with a positive approach regardless of any previous failures.

Inmates who accept their situation and who "get on with their life" have a tendency to do far better than those who harbor ill feelings about past events or behavior.

Is it a sign of weakness to be positive? There are some individuals who feel that they are "selling out." They think that they appear "soft" if they let go of anger or do good for others. Some individuals believe that it is a sign of weakness to learn or simplify their lives.

In short, some individuals perceive positive outlooks as being weak. However, they mistakenly use negativity as a coping tool.

Negative individuals are also prone to relapse and have a lower rate of breaking old and unproductive habits. They are limiting their internal freedom.

Positive people recover more quickly. Use your time as a powerful period of self-reflection and you will see that positive qualities are signs of strength.

Positive Attitude, Positive Thinking, Positive Talking

Inmates with positive thoughts, positive words, and positive actions and a wide group of positive acquaintances tend to cope better. They hold positive qualities during incarceration and also when they return home to their families.

Positive direction is momentum that permits individuals to do far better than others. They set goals and are successful in reaching them. The secret of goal setting is not to let failures or mistakes obstruct your goal. Move toward the goal regardless of any setback. Ten steps forward and two steps back is, in reality, eight steps ahead.

Goal setters usually have multiple goals and do not toss out their goals because they "failed" to do everything exactly right. They know that they can learn from setbacks.

One goal might be to read one good book every month. Another goal might be to learn another language. Lifting weights and working out three times a week is a goal. Each goal is different.

If your entire "world" rides on one change or goal, it might be devastating when the natural process of change does not meet personal linear expectations.

Change is like a dance with forward and backwards movement. Ten steps forward and two steps back is still…eight steps ahead of where you were.

Words from a brother...

When you say a negative word, it sticks into your mind and you believe it. Once you hear it, you act upon it; and you send that out like a radio signal, a vibration.

Most prison guards know that they have authority over you and they use that to push your buttons. The thing is that GOGI has introduced the technique called the LIGHTSWITCH. You have power over yourself; you have power over your brain.

Pause before you react. Turn on the light switch. That negative vibe will be transferred to a positive one. When you are negative you give them power over you.

Being the BOSS OF YOUR BRAIN... It all starts with the mind. If you think it, you can be it. It is not easy but it IS possible. Think positive. Get your THREE KEYS. It is not easy -- it is an acquired practice.

Coach DJ talks to kids attending DeAnza College
in Inglewood, California.

HOW TO MASTER POSITIVE TWA

STEP 1) AWARENESS – Take a moment to imagine what it would be like if you controlled your internal world to such an extent that you were perpetually positive. Become acutely aware of when you are positive and when you are negative.

The fact is, you cannot think positively and speak negatively. You cannot speak negatively and have positive actions.

And, repeated thoughts, words and actions become well-worn neurological habits. The well-worn neurological habits bypass conscious thought and become an intuitive automatic reaction.

Become highly aware of what you think, what words you use, and the actions you take. Become aware of what others hear comes out of your mouth and how they might interpret your communication.

With AWARENESS you are on your way to escaping the "auto pilot" cycle of negativity.

STEP 2) PAUSE *BEFORE* YOU SPEAK - Before you say anything, pause and consider the thoughts, words and actions that you are about to choose.

Words pop into in your mind as thoughts before you say them. Take charge of the thoughts and demand that they get reformulated, morphed, modified, changed, swapped into positive words.

Pause before speak and pause before you respond. Take in feedback from others about the words that you have chosen. How are people responding to your positive, or negative, words and actions?

Think about those individuals who say that they "are only speaking the truth." Perhaps they should consider how much of their communication is actually the truth and then focus on the message of their words. Do you really need to point out the entire negative? Does it really do any good to complain and point out flaws?

Consider that your negative "truth" is really just your negative experience or opinion. Your truth is not necessarily their truth. Will your negative thoughts, words and actions "change" them? Unlikely.

There might be a guard who is a jerk most of the time. You can say that he is a jerk. You can have negative thoughts, negative words and even negative actions towards this negative guard. You can be caught in his negative loop or you can refocus on someone, something, or some thoughts that are more positive.

Take the power out of the other person's hands and claim responsibility for your positive experiences.

> *"He's such an idiot," is just as truthful as "He's acted smarter before."*
> **Coach Taylor**

STEP 3) SLOW DOWN - Don't rush to think, speak or act. Very few things in life require immediate responses and actions. Most situations in our life would be better managed if we took a bit more time in reacting. There is a popular technique of counting to 10 before you utter a word or engage in an action. Use this technique if it helps.

Your communication becomes purposeful and positive when you slow down. Interestingly enough, people who use pauses and contemplative thought in their lives are often considered to appear "smarter" or "well educated" or "grounded."

Slowing down is not automatic and reactionary. Slowing down is purposeful and precise.

STEP 4) OBSERVE - When you speak to someone, watch their reactions. When they speak you can observe their process of thought. Look at the entire exchange of communication. Are your words having the effect you intended? If not, stop talking.

Words from a brother

From what I have learned, there are two parts of a conversation that are very important. The first part is the listening. You have to listen because if you talk while the speaker is talking you are going to miss something. Listen.

And speak clearly, if you are the speaker. Focus on your words so they come across with the meaning you want. If I talk crazy to you, then you are going to talk crazy to me. You are goin to take what I say with one thing on the mind...defend.

Everything goes back to the breathing... try listening when you can relax. Analyze what is being said. Actions and words follow thoughts and feelings. Listen and you will learn. This is not just for inmates. This is for anyone.

That is the important thing. Anybody can use this information and become a better speaker, and you also become a better listener.

Actually, I learned this from Coach Taylor. Listen and speak slowly.

THINK ABOUT IT

Reflect on the following phrases. Which phrases are used by successful people?

NEGATIVE SELF TALK	POSITIVE SELF TALK
I can't, won't, shouldn't, wouldn't.	I WILL
I won't, can't, shouldn't, wouldn't.	I WANT to
I don't care, it's not my problem, it's not my fault.	I CARE
It's too tough, cant' be done, won't happen.	IT'S TOUGH, but I WILL
I am stupid, it's not going to happen.	I AM SMART
I am an idiot, it's not for me, I can't do it.	I CAN do it
I don't want to do it, I can't, won't, never will.	I WANT to do it
I am a loser, the odds are against me.	I AM a WINNER!

The Eyes in the Mirror

I may appear "free" to family and friends. Yet, my prison walls relentlessly reconstruct themselves as quickly as I break them down. Another brick magically appears for every one that I remove. Sometimes the journey inward feels impossible. It seems like a futile attempt to battle an unwavering torrent of obstacles.

One day I expressed my weariness to Coach DJ. He told me of a long stretch he did in SHU University, the Special Housing Unit.

There was not a soul with whom to share his torment as month after month in solitary passed by. He felt that he was at the lowest point that he could be.

He needed someone to talk to and decided to look in the mirror. The man in the mirror was his best - and only - option.

He took a few sheets of toilet paper and held it over the mirror image of his mouth so that image of two watchful eyes would be there – listening. Just a set of worn and soulful eyes...listening as words of anguish poured forth.

The man in the SHU simply needed another soul with whom to converse.

Occasionally, the advice of friends irritates my sensibilities. Or a helpful conversation with God seems beyond my grasp. And sometimes I catch a glimpse of my eyes looking back at me from a mirror's reflection. That is when I am reminded that I have all the compassion I need to make it through another day.

Coach Taylor

REFLECTION

What words do you use to describe your wife or girlfriend? When you speak to your friends about your mate, are you being critical or complimentary? What about when you talk about your best friend? Your education?

What words do you use choose to describe your job? How do you describe your meals? Your health? Your family?

How do you put into words what you think about your future? Today? Your past? Your parents? Your boss? Your supervisor? Your past mistakes? Prospects for your future?

Focus on the areas of your life using POSITIVE TWA.

Create positive thoughts, replacing the negative and unproductive opinions and impressions with a focus on positive. Acknowledge three positive things about yourself that you can focus on and emphasize. Choose positive words. Focus on positive actions.

Remember...

Lasting change is generally gradual and occurs over a stretch of time. Become aware of your thoughts. Be attentive to your words. Pause before taking actions.

POSITIVE TWA will strengthen you as you move forward. Inch your way towards thought, positive talk and note its effect on your choice of actions.

POSITIVE TWA leads to positive character, positive experience with others, and a positive experience in your life.

WATCH OTHERS

Listen to others. People seem to talk as though they are on "auto pilot" and do not think before they speak. Positive talkers are usually more careful in their choice of words. They often speak less and have more control over their thoughts, emotions and words.

You are likely to discover vital information when observing others. Extra information gives you a powerful focal point. You can manage and direct your reactions with positive word choices.

POSITIVE TWA permits you to create the kind of experience which supports your internal freedom. POSITIVE TWA is a powerful tool for freedom before your release.

CONSIDER THIS...

POSITIVE TWA
will keep you
aware of your
negative and
positive thoughts
and words.

POSITIVE TWA
helps put you
in the driver's
seat and helps
you take your
thoughts off
"auto pilot."

POSITIVE TWA
In Action

MIKE QUITS SMOKING WEED

Mike faced many troubling thoughts when he decided to quit smoking weed. He wanted to be very mindful of his thought patterns.

His thoughts undoubtedly end up as actions because that is how the human brain works. Every action begins with a thought.

Mike had the idea to have just one hit. This thought created a new thought. "I am such a loser for not being able to quit."

The thoughts propelled him into other thoughts. "But it sure smells good," he remembered. "I get so relaxed and it helps me to chill out."

Mike needed to take control and let POSITIVE TWA work for him. He remembered the theory of POSITIVE TWA. He could use the tool of POSITIVE TWA at any time to take control of his thoughts and behavior.

He knew that his life was up to him no matter how many thoughts flooded his mind.

He remembered his POSITIVE personal qualities. Mike took steps to take control over his thoughts and actions.

1) Mike creates his own internal positive attitude. He thinks of the positive aspects in his life. He thinks of his talents. He focuses on his future. The present is going to get him into trouble. The future is where he will find strength to move forward.

2) Mike has the ability to use the FIVE SECOND LIGHTSWITCH to exchange potentially destructive thinking for positive thinking. He is no longer a slave to his old habits.

3) Mike begins to choose positive words when he thinks about his positive attributes. He CAN and WILL succeed.

He has succeeded in the past. He will succeed in the future. He begins to use powerful words like CAN and WILL. These words influence his actions.

WHY POSITIVE TWA WORKS

POSITIVE TWA works on the principal that negative thoughts and words bring negative results — and positive thoughts and words bring positive results.

Shape POSITIVE TWA into natural habits and you will find an easier path toward success in every area of your life.

The kind of future that you wish for yourself is within reach. You will notice that you have become more powerful.

Use POSITIVE TWA in your communication. Others will begin to behave more constructively. Your positive presence supports change in your surroundings.

OBSERVE YOURSELF AND OTHERS...

Notice that the pace quickens when individuals respond negatively. Those who are slower to react are more attentive in their responses.

Observe the ratio of negative and positive words that you use. Remember that three positive thoughts outweigh a single negative thought.

Anytime that you think, "I can't," add "but I can do something else." Add "I have accomplished many things but maybe not this one."

Keep adding positive thoughts. What are your positive qualities?

READ

There are tons and tons of books available about the lives of successful individuals. In each case, you will find that these individuals are POSITIVE, not negative, about any situation to which they may find themselves. READ, READ, READ biographies, autobiographies, "how-to" books.....anything that supports your POSITIVE TWA.

No Such Thing as Failure

Teachers, administrators, probation officers and even parents often ask the question "Why do the kids act differently when they are with you?" They are perplexed with the "instant" behavioral changes in the seemingly "impossible" children.

Frankly, I believe success with troubled kids stems from quick identification and support of their positive qualities.

Every individual has positive qualities, which can be nurtured. They can outshine their challenges regardless of age, race, beliefs or level of crimes.

I look for the positive in every person then compliment, support and acknowledge these qualities every time I see them.

THERE IS NO ROOM FOR FAILURE WHEN YOU FOCUS ON SUCCESS.

Coach Taylor

The People of GOGI

Coach DJ taking it easy on the FREE side of the fence.

<u>Anyone</u> can find Internal Freedom. Anyone!

Words of Wisdom

"Experience is never at fault; it is only your judgment that is in error, in promising itself such results from experience as are not caused by our experiments. For having given a beginning, what follows from it must necessarily be a natural development of such a beginning, unless it has been subject to a contrary influence, while, if it is affected by any contrary influence, the result which ought to follow from the aforesaid beginning, will be found to partake of this contrary influence in a greater or lesser degree in proportion as the said influence is more or less powerful than the aforesaid beginning."

Leonardo da Vinci
Philosophy, Codie Atlantico 44.b

*In other words . . . go easy on yourself during the inevitable obstacles experienced in this existence called life. Even individuals nearly 2000 years ago struggled with what to make of life's challenges.

Coach Taylor

CHAPTER NINE
REALITY CHECK

It would be nice if change happened immediately and without relapsing into old behaviors. But change can be a slow process of "two steps forward, one step back." Change may also require constant monitoring until the new habits become automatic.

The unfortunate aspect of our society today is that we go for quick fixes and often give up on our goals during the "one step back" part of the change process.

An individual might think, "I promised myself that this time would be different and I failed," or "Obviously, I can never change." They choose not to believe in themselves and are burdened with evidence that they cannot make changes in their behavior.

They might argue, saying, "It's prison. Change is impossible in a place like this," or, "If the situation was more supportive I WOULD change."

The point is that everyone has a different insight and experience about the process of change. Your perception develops over time. And, your experiences create the realities that you experience.

There is no need to feel low or get angry at the world if you "relapse" into old behaviors or beliefs. While it may not be optimal, you can really think of falling back into old behavior and as a visit down memory lane or a place that you do not care to remain. Get yourself out of there as soon as possible.

It's quite probable that you will recover from relinquishing control of your life, and get yourself back into the driver's seat. You can become the boss again. You can create your life instead of old habits creating the same results.

Words from a brother...

Relapse, to my understanding, is a returning behavior that you said you were going to stop.

I think people relapse because they look too far into the future. People relapse because of anger, out of frustration, or loneliness.

When someone is uncomfortable, they need to get out of reality and go where they are comfortable which is the far side. This is why people relapse.

This may sound crazy but I find comfort from going into myself. That is my refuge, in my internal being. I'm not worrying about relapse. It is not even on my list. I am serious.

One day I was told to make a list of my good things of my week and the bad things of my week. When it was my turn to read my list I only read my good parts. When asked about my bad list, I said, "That is the past. It plays no part in my life right now. Today, everything is perfect."

No, I am not going to relapse or think about a bad week. I am going to spend my time with my list of good.

I am comfortable with myself. I am not dis-easy any more.

Words from a brother...

That's what kills me, right there. I am not fueled by anger and resentment. I am a grown man, and I can show my feelings to those who are on my same frequency. That is why I have not been broken, shaken or stirred.

There are some individuals who try to test the water and try to talk about what I am doing for me. I listen to them and what they have to say. I spoke in calm, measured tones. I gave them what I have inside me. When I spoke of my reputation, they were compelled to listen without saying one word. They understood that I do this for me and nobody else. This is what I call my sign of true God-given strength.

But you know what, when I get cats one-on-one, I tell them what I am doing, they would come up to me at my bunk. They didn't want to be seen coming up to me in a crowd cuz they were worried about the penitentiary ego. The Ego has no bearing on me. They were still worried. When I said to them if I get out of here the same way I came in I'm fucked. I gotta do something.

Now I say, come as you are. The important thing is, if you reading these words do not leave as you came.

REALITY CHECK will:

- Help you understand that "ten steps forward and two steps back" is a part of the process of most change.

- Help you lighten up on self-criticism and self-blame with the understanding that you can return to your path after a relapse.

- Help you master your process of change and acknowledge that even if it is slow it may also lead toward lasting freedom.

The People of GOGI

Coach Wanda teaches at-risk kids the GOGI concepts.

THE TRUTH IS. . .

REALITY CHECK
allows you to remain positive
about the changes that you
make in your life.

REALITY CHECK
provides you with a
"walk down memory lane,"
gently reminding you
of places that you do not wish
to return, habits that you
are leaving behind, and
attitudes and actions that
no longer work in
your best interest.

HOW DOES REALITY CHECK WORK?

You can focus on the end objective when you understand that change is not always linear or experienced immediately. Set aside any momentary step backward as being an old or unfavorable way of being or behaving.

Think of it like a needle and thread that weaves two pieces of fabric together. The needle pulls the thread forward, and then turns back and loops over previously traveled territory before moving forward again.

Eventually, the fabric is sewn together. It benefits from a "relapse" of looping over the same sections of fabric it covered previously.

It is not an act of failure for the needle to loop over previously sewn fabric.

Move forward in the larger scheme of things. Think of those few steps back as visiting a place where you no longer reside or want to be.

Let this temporary visit remind you of your significant changes and progress. Continue the delicate dance of restructuring your neurological habits.

ADDED BENEFITS OF REALITY CHECK

It is likely that any relapse of behavior will be shorter, not likely to be repeated, and easier to overcome when you take on the attitude of REALITY CHECK.

HERE'S WHY REALITY CHECK WORKS...

You might label yourself incapable of EVER achieving your objective if you fall into old patterns of behavior and regard yourself as a "loser." Saying "I am a mess up" is a global negative statement. Try saying, "I messed up right now and I won't mess up later."

Acknowledge that behavior is something that you can control. Relapse is a temporary visit to a place that you no longer live. You can speedily regain control of the steering wheel of your life.

HOW TO DO THE <u>REALITY CHECK</u> TECHNIQUE

You control your actions when you control your thoughts. A major tool in controlling your thoughts is REALITY CHECK. It is a simple way to regain control.

Here are the straightforward steps to REALITY CHECK.

STEP 1) REALIZE THAT YOU BACKTRACKED - You must realize, recognize and admit to yourself that you have returned to an old belief or behavior. Admitting your situation is the first step to returning to your desired path.

STEP 2) MEMORY LANE - Understand, and truly believe, that an old behavior is a momentary visit down "memory lane." It is not where you want to remain.

STEP 3) FORWARD BENEFITS - Focus on the benefits of change before you get sucked into believing that this old place holds anything good for you. Ask yourself why you wanted to change in the first place. What do you need to do right now to continue moving forward?

STEP 4) RECOVERY - Grab the wheel of the car, even if you are going 90 miles an hour down a slippery slope. You can slow down with BELLY BREATHING. Get back into control by using the tools that you have learned.

STEP 5) RECOGNIZE - Recognize that only you are BOSS OF YOUR BRAIN. Focus on BELLY BREATHING. Use the FIVE SECOND LIGHTSWITCH to bring in new thoughts. Use WHAT IF? to jump start your actions. Focus on POSITIVE TWA.

Words from a brother...

This is who I am today. I am going to try again tomorrow. The important thing is to never feel over confident. Just confident. Use the tools. Network.

Talk to yourself in the mirror if you need to look someone in the eye. Tell someone your problems. That is what I do. If I am by my damn self, and I need to talk to somebody. It may sound funny. It's kinda funny. It is funny. But it works.

The thing is, we are trying to save ourselves, one person at a time. I can't save you. The only thing I can do is tell you what I am doing to save myself.

That is all I can do. Nothing more.

CONSIDER THIS...

REALITY CHECK

is a powerful way to get back on track with your new beliefs and behaviors.

REALITY CHECK

helps remind you of what you really want by allowing you to temporarily visit a place that you no longer belong.

REALITY CHECK

sees a return to old behavior as a walk down memory lane and not as a lasting turn of events or failure.

THINK ABOUT IT

Sometimes your negative or "bad" habits seem impossible to change. People seem to push your buttons.

Sometimes you are so tired, run down, or discouraged that a slip backwards seems unavoidable. It may seem impossible to give up an unconstructive habit no matter how better your life would be.

Take a moment to reflect on some habits that you tried to change. It is likely that you did not quit if you felt that you were being successful in your efforts.

It is likely that you started to spiral downward, tossed your hands into the air, and claimed that the habit was in control of you. Or, worse yet, that you never really wanted to give up the habit.

It is likely that you gave up on change when you felt that you had failed or had a relapse. People usually give up prematurely when doing the 10 steps forward and 2 steps back dance of change.

Sometimes, lasting change happens slowly. We all fall down. Just keep moving forward. And, go easy on yourself. Just get up quickly and put one foot in front of the next.

WATCH OTHERS

Watch others who attempt to break habits. From observation of the steps they take to break a habit, you might notice that the process is not so easy.

First, individuals may start out by making grandiose proclamations about their goal. Strong statements make it seem like the challenge will be easy to overcome.

Little by little, they face temptations that are hard to resist. Later, they make a convincing list of reasons why they are not meeting their goal. Finally, blaming another person or situation starts the cycle over again.

Tread lightly

Individuals who are successful in breaking habits tend to tread lightly on the issue of their addiction or bad habits. They do not believe that they are invincible. They acknowledge their human frailty when weaknesses surface in the form of old behaviors.

Be gentle with yourself during the process of change. Notice when you feel strong enough to distance yourself from your bad habits.

It's difficult to soar with the eagles when you hang with the turkeys.
Anonymous

Take a moment to reflect on what happens when you strongly reinforce new behaviors. With whom do you spend time? What you are thinking and how do you feel? Repeat positive influences as often as you can. Hang with positive people. Being with positive people allows you access to positive words, actions, and conversations.

Walk away from negativity. Read positive materials. Say positive things. Think positive thoughts. Positive invites more positive into your life. Have a goal to break a habit. Goals help you from being overwhelmed by a momentary, mindless return to a place that you no longer want to be. Place yourself in a supportive environment as often as possible.

People who ultimately change bad habits are those who keep moving forward, even after a setback.

The People of GOGI

Coach DJ and Coach Alex receive an award from Principal Brownlee for GOGI's involvement in the Inglewood, CA school district.

```
┌─────────────────────────────────────────┐
│                                         │
│          REALITY CHECK                  │
│           In Action                     │
│                                         │
└─────────────────────────────────────────┘
```

MIKE QUITS SMOKING WEED

Let's visit our friend, Mike, who has been smoking weed with his brothers since he was 9 years old. He is now 27 years old and has been in trouble with the law since he was 12 for breaking into homes and stealing to get money to buy weed.

One of the reasons that he smokes is because he does not know how to control his anger. Smoking calms him. All his troubles seem to go away when he is high. Sometimes he gets so angry that he loses control over his thoughts and actions. Mike knows that he needs to control his anger and quit smoking, but it all seems beyond his control.

Mike just had a fight with his girlfriend. He storms out and heads to his buddy's house. There are several guys there, smoking. His thoughts drift to "Maybe just one hit.'

Let's say Mike forgot to do the BELLY BREATHING. He forgot THE FIVE SECOND LIGHTSWITCH. He ignores his WHAT IF? questions or any other technique that can strengthen his ability to change.

Let's say that he sits down with his buddies and gets higher than he has been in months. Eventually he returns home to a disgusted girlfriend and he feels like a loser again.

262PRISON: GETTING OUT BY GOING IN - By Coach Taylor

REALITY CHECK IN ACTION

1) REALIZE THAT YOU BACKTRACKED - First, Mike interprets the night's events as backtracking, and not as a permanent place to where he has returned.

He backtracked for 8 hours. He realizes that he stayed away from weed for hundreds of hours prior. One hundred hours forward, eight hours back. He reminds himself that he has a commitment to break the habit.

2) MEMORY LANE - A critical element of this technique is for Mike to understand, and truly believe that what he experienced is an old behavior or belief. It is a mindless return to a place that he no longer wants to be. It is similar to visiting an old school after you have long graduated.

3) FORWARD BENEFITS - Before Mike gets sucked into believing that getting high holds anything good for him, he begins to focus on the benefits of change.

He remembers why he wanted to change and all the times that he was able to say no. He remembers that he is capable of doing things differently. To remain on track, he spends less time thinking about what he has done and more time on what to do right now.

4)   RECOVERY - Mike does whatever it takes to return to a positive mental state. He knows that a positive mental state results in positive behavior. When his girlfriend expresses anger, he calmly reminds her why he is committed to breaking the habit and what the benefits are.

He asks for her support to help him return to his desired behavior. He calls his friend and tells him that it was great to spend time with him. He tells his friend not to take it personally if he does not show up for a while. He needs to get high less often — and eventually quit for good.

5)   RECOGNIZE - Most importantly, Mike can go easy on judging himself. He knows that it can take a long time to change a habit.

Regardless of how long it is going to take, he commits to moving forward. Mike does not take his eyes off the long-term benefit of changing his short-term reactions.

WHY IT WORKS

REALITY CHECK is a speedy recovery technique. It empowers you to have a REALITY CHECK when you temporarily return to old and unproductive way of believing or behaving.

Taking the time to get a REALITY CHECK will permit you a realistic perspective on the change process. You can see the distance that you have traveled thus far.

You can focus on all the good that has come out of your changes so far. You can review your accomplishments, refocus on them, and know that they are your key to regaining forward momentum once again.

If you go easy on yourself through the process of a reality check, your commitment will strengthen. Look at relapse as a temporary visit to a place that you no longer wish to be, and you will return quicker to the desired behavior.

OBSERVE OTHERS...

Notice the behavior of others. When people give up on a new habit, take notice if it happened when they had a relapse?

When you observe others, you are less likely to wallow in self-pity. This does not mean to observe others and blame them for your problems. It means observe and speak with others who have changed a habit, modified a behavior, or reached a goal.

Observing others might mean reading a biography of someone who overcame all odds, or speaking with someone who has risen above addictions.

Also, observe yourself…

When you slide back into old ways of behaving or old beliefs you can use REALITY CHECK to get yourself back on track.

You can also observe your thought patterns, and modify them with a more realistic interpretation of your progress.

You will feel powerless if you think that your thoughts are beyond your control, or when you abdicate your right for an amazing life. The more that you know about yourself the more likely you are to make strong and positive decisions.

By observing, truly observing the causes and the effects of your behavior you will undoubtedly feel compelled to walk as far from bad habits as possible.

Get to know yourself. Strengthen yourself from the inside outward. Observe yourself and listen to that still and small voice which only can be heard when you are silent and breathe.

Reach for the Top

I remember a hiking trip I took to Hawaii. Hiking to the top of mountains sounded great, but there were obstacles in the way of my rise to the top. The ground was soggy, making it squishy to walk. Rain was pending and I was under-protected. The light was dimming making the path difficult to see.

My guide/friend and I were exhausted and, frankly, quite tired of each other's company. I was not really having the fun that I had envisioned for the trip — I was hungry, thirsty, and discouraged.

Coach Taylor hiking to the top of the mountain in Hawaii.

Only by keeping my focus on the destination was the pain of the journey diminished.

My eyes were weary when I reached the top of the volcanic mountain. Yet my soul soared as I looked out at ocean that stretched as far as I could see. The struggle has long been forgotten but I still have the pictures of my triumphant journey to the volcanic mountain top in Hawaii.

Coach Taylor

Note: No one truly gets to the top without effort.

CHAPTER TEN

THE ULTIMATE FREEDOM

TOOLS FOR A GREAT FUTURE

You are not exactly the same individual that you were yesterday. Tomorrow you will not be exactly the same person as you are today.

We may not detect subtle changes that nudge us right or left on life's uncertain crossroads. Changes are often incremental and continual. You create new possibilities as you process each new bit of information, thought or experience. Accumulation of positive information eventually bears the fruit of that tree.

It seems like there needs to be a critical mass of information or experience for a new reality to set in place. You do not go to the gym one time and expect muscles to pop out like a cartoon. Similarly, internal freedom is the result of an accumulation of consistent effort over a period of time.

It is almost impossible to note subtle changes. Good intentions may not have a chance to take root and grow, especially in fast paced, instant-gratification society.

We seek immediate answers, quick cash, lotto numbers, mega million numbers, magic pills, a silver bullet, or a faster way to move through life.

We abdicate our right to create magnificent lives, irrespective of where we live them, when we mistakenly look outside ourselves.

Certain restrictions apply to how fast you can physically move through life during incarceration.

You have a precious and valuable opportunity in this imposed slowdown. You have the opportunity to get out of the human prison and find a rare and powerful freedom. The journey inward is life long.

I do not recall meeting or hearing about any individual who found an internal freedom that would effortlessly last a lifetime.

Even in a religious awakening or enlightenment, there is still the need for constant maintenance of the inward journey. There is a relentless practice of shedding moral perceptions in order to travel inward where the soul resides.

Take advantage of your incarceration and make this thing called life work for you. Internal freedom is a natural steps that can be included as a part of your daily living.

Words from a brother…

Give it to me right now. Fast cash, magic pill, lucky lotto, whatever it might be. Everyone wants the easy way out. No one wants to sweat, earn, me included. I didn't want to do none of that.

But now, when I became free, something happened. I could not wait to go home to do good. But before I went home to start going good, I started doing good to my self by starting to do good to myself. I started to go to classes and not just the hobby craft classes.

I took classes to feed my spirit. Now I feel that I am being a good human being.

I am free, like I said before, before they freed me, I am free.

I know that I do not have power over anyone reading these words on what you do. The only thing I would like is for you to feel how I feel today. That's all I want.

With that right there, you will have the magic button, the magic super bullet, and the lucky lotto numbers. It will not be in that form, but it will mean more. It means much more.

We have discussed the following steps earlier in the book. This should be a reminder for you to keep a watchful eye for when and how they show up in daily experiences.

LET GO

Decide to free yourself and you will LET GO of what keeps you from a joyful existence. You will find a way to move beyond old resentments, anger, fear, and unpleasant memories that imprison you.

You will find that money, fame, prestige, position, activities and chatter about the motivations of others are obstacles to your freedom.

For some individuals, permission to LET GO and welcome internal freedom comes from a secular (religious) experience.

For some, it is facilitated by a spiritual experience, which may come from meditation or yoga.

For some, LET GO comes from accumulated data that is presented in books. For some individuals, it is volunteer work, or focusing on assisting others which permits them to experience LET GO.

For some individuals, LET GO happens when there is no room to go down further into depression and LET GO is the their only hope for living.

LET GO lights the path in the journey to internal freedom.

FORGIVENESS

You will notice the act of FORGIVENESS, of self and of others. Along the path toward internal freedom there will come a natural, and perhaps effortless, forgiveness. Somewhere along the journey, you will begin to soften your anger, resentment, bitterness, rage and retaliation.

You will come to understand that the longer you hold on to events and actions of the past, it is becomes more difficult to move away from them.

When you enter a state of FORGIVENESS, you are able to travel freely and unload the "baggage." Those who you might find offensive are no longer attached to you or your thoughts. You can let them fend for themselves.

Also, in this process of internal freedom, there will come a moment when you truly forgive yourself for your own humanness.

You will leave behind the heavy load of thinking that you do not have potential for improvement or increased levels of joy and internal freedom.

FORGIVENESS of self will permit you to walk beyond the actions and thoughts of the past into a far brighter future.

You limit new and different possibilities when you define yourself by prior actions or reactions. To permit FORGIVENESS of self also permits new possibilities.

RESPONSIBILITY

The final stage on your journey toward internal freedom is the finest, most empowering experience.

It is the art of personal RESPONSIBILITY.

You may not feel in control of anything in your life. However, you are completely and totally in control of how you act, re-act, and think about events and situations.

In fact, the most out-of-control and unhappy individuals are those who attempt to control their loved ones. Acting on internal fears, they exert control over their environment by creating rules for those around them.

Internal freedom correlates to your level of personal RESPONSIBILITY.

With internal freedom, you are not likely say "You make me mad," or "If you would just…" Actions or reactions of others do not control the truly free individual.

Internally free individuals assume and welcome total RESPONSIBILITY into their lives.

Here is an excerpt from the book "Deep and Simple" written by my friend, Bo Lozoff:

> "... our community is exactly where we are at every moment during the day; exactly whom life places in front of us at any time. That's the whole point. That idiot, that lecher, the con, the cop, the snitch, the boss who drives us up the wall, the windbag politician on TV – everyone we see, hear, or meet must be respected as a brother or sister on the path, even if they have no idea there is such a thing as a path.
>
> Clearly, this practice of Community is not for cowards; it's challenging and confusing, and it's fulltime...."

Everyone is your community. Everyone is on the path. You will only become as free as your muscles of personal RESPONSIBILITY permit you.

Words from a brother...

Responsibility for our self is a continual practice—on a daily basis. If you just practice these simple tasks, these simple practices, you will become a more responsible employee, father, friend, and neighbor.

You will be led to a responsible life. You will meet and befriend responsible people. Your personal responsibility will be taken care of. You will be that husband to your wife. You will pay your bills on time. You won't go to jail or prison any more.

Freedom is responsibility. Responsibility is freedom.

I choose not to give my freedom or my responsibility away to anyone.

Under the laws now, they will take your freedom away for a long time. The thing is use BOSS OF YOUR BRAIN, BELLY BREATHING, FIVE SECOND LIGHTSWITCH, POSITIVE TWA, WHAT IF?, REALITY CHECK. They are right there, and really really important.

If you don't understand the rules, you will go to prison. If you are a hot tempered and you get the "fuckits" don't let someone else be the boss of your brain. Get in a situation where you can walk away. It is acting responsibly. People with anger issues? They are to be extra careful. Proceed with caution. Use the FIVE SECOND LIGHTSWITCH, BELLY BREATHING. Use it all.

WORDS TO WATCH.....

Disempowering sentences include the following:
"It wasn't my fault…"
"No one will hire an ex-con at anything more
than slave labor wages."
"The system…."
"The judge…"
"The warden…"
"The guards…"
"The walls…"
"No one understands."
"It's never going to change."
"He has it out for me."
"She makes me so mad."
"He gave me no choice."
"He pissed me off."
"They disrespected me."
"The system works against a guy like me."
"No one can win in a place like this."
"I have to respond or they will think I am soft."
"I can't let him talk to me that way."

RESPONSIBILITY allows you to disconnect from the suction cup of emotional control and from others that take away your freedom. These suction cups attach to you, and leave you powerless and imprisoned.

Do not let anyone's behavior, thoughts, actions or reactions alter your course. You must assume total RESPONSIBILITY if you desire internal freedom.

LET GO, FORGIVENESS and RESPONSIBILITY are TOOLS that complement the experiences in this book. They help to light your way on your journey toward internal freedom.

Only you can set yourself free

Right now, you hold the keys to your internal freedom. You may not totally believe it. By applying these new tools, you can mold and shape your life experience.

Hold these tools as a core component of who you are and how you live in this world. You will discover how easily change can take place.

These tools have the potential to dramatically improve your life, seemingly overnight. In other cases, it will take months or years to find a way into your core. No matter how long it takes, these tools are yours to use as you see fit.

You will pick up new information each time you review this book. Repeat the weekly process as many times as you wish. Practicing the techniques will help you to powerfully and positively rework your life. Even if you think that you "got" the information, reread the material and take more notes. Like a pro athlete, there is only good which can come from practicing over and over and over again.

> **The simple truth? You are an amazing, powerful force for good, waiting for permission to embrace your internal freedom. Give yourself that permission right now. No one will do it for you. Freedom is yours to claim and to build upon through your journey inward. GETTING OUT of prison BY GOING IN to your internal freedom is your right and privilege.**

I want to share with you one of my favorite quotes. It is buried within the gems sprinkled throughout "We're all Doing Time."

> *...That's really the whole thing in a nutshell: we have so little power, really, that it's ridiculous. And yet, the way the Universe is designed, it's all just waiting for that insignificant little spark from our hearts to set all the beauty and truth in motion, spinning like a top. It's so unimaginably perfect! Powerlessness forces us to be humble, yet when we recognize who we really are in the big scheme of things, we become enlightened and suddenly we have access to all the power in the universe."*

A Thought from Coach. . .

May God bless you on your journey inward to the only lasting freedom available to mankind. I know this to be true, getting out by going in is a universal experience of internal freedom. It is waiting for the spark deep inside you to fuel its fire within.

Continue your journey inward. I will keep you in my prayers that you remain committed to your internal freedom. I ask that you keep me in your prayers as well.

My dedication to this journey inward is undying and relentless but not absent struggle and heartbreak.

If I feel alone in my journey, the trail might seem uncertain and the path unclear. I often recall my favorite Sufi saying:

"After all this time, the sun has never said to the earth... you owe me."

Let your light shine freely before men. When we love each other in that manner, it lights up the entire world.

After tossing many untruths aside the objective of finding internal freedom is within reach. With any luck, you will discover that the bars of internal imprisonment are actually an illusion.

I have this wonderful verse in my home:

> *It is better to light a candle*
> *than to curse the darkness.*
> *Anonymous*

Light the candle within you. Let it glow and grow with awareness. It leads to new insights, which leads to new behaviors.

Once your candle burns brightly, you can help others to become conscious of their candle. With enough of us helping each other, we can light up the entire world.

Please return to the first page and read the entire book again. And then one more time. You will be amazed at the new information that you learn or pick up from a second, third or fourth reading.

Much love, respect and support for your journey.

Coach Taylor at the GOGI office.

GETTING OUT BY GOING IN
Freedom Before Your Release

....

Personal Tools For Internal Freedom
Help you to. . .

LET GO, FORGIVE & CLAIM RESPONSIBILITY

BOSS OF YOUR BRAIN allows you to take control of all your thoughts and actions.

BELLY BREATHING allows you to take control of your entire body.

FIVE SECOND LIGHTSWITCH allows you to stop and think before you act.

WHAT IF? allows you to think from a powerful and positive perspective.

POSITIVE TWA
(Thoughts, Words, Actions)
TWA are three keys that allows you to control your thoughts, word, and actions.

REALITY CHECK allows you to accept the process of change more fully.

 **GETTING OUT BY GOING IN**
Inmate testimonials...

Over the period of 5 years, the GOGI 6-week course was offered to more than 600 inmate participants. At the end of the class, each participant was invited to express their ideas & thoughts about what they learned. Here is what they had to say. <u>Note</u>: *Originals are on file in the GOGI office.*

The class helps the mind and the way I feel....... wonderful.... and to relax. It has helped me to listen and see both sides of an argument. Waiting five seconds can help you not to rush into things.
S. W.

The class has helped me deal with situations in a positive way and stay in control. It has helped me to listen and see both sides of an argument. Waiting five seconds can help you not to rush into things.
L. Y.

I think it's gonna be easier for me to allow people to do their thing without me trying to control it and I'm gonna take care of my own business.
M. C.

This course has helped me in every possible way...I have come a long way. This course has made a profound change in how I interact with others. I am very grateful for this course.
G

The course gives people a chance to put together and get ideas from one another. Just talking about it helps.
Anonymous

It has made me focus on who I am and what is important I am generous, smart and easy going, which makes me feel great! Listening is the best technique. This course gives all people a chance to look inside first and then to look outside.
Anonymous

It's useful for me to understand how to control the body, mind and spirit. For my family, it's good to have better communication and to be more patient.
Anonymous

It is always good to understand "why" it is and "what" it is. I can utilize substituting new habits for older ones. It has made me more confident.
D. A.

All the techniques are helpful to me and would help my family. The course is helpful and keeps me coming back (to the workshop) again.
E. A. A.

It has shown me how to block negativity out of my life. It was helpful to learn the differences in the way the brain functions. The course helped me get some positive input on life.
D. J.

Relaxation teaches me not to get emotional to breath and think before acting. It helped me to focus on me goals and to keep a positive outlook on things. It helps me to control my emotions through concentration of my mind. Coach Taylor is a wonderful listener as well as a very positive person who helps you with your ideas and maked them a reality.
D. A.

This course has been very positive and uplifting to me. I have learned how to channel my anger inwards and used that energy into creativity. I learned to pay attention and be aware of every detail. It has helped me, so I'm sure it will be beneficial to others.
A. G.

This course was helpful to me personally and I can share the good experiences, especially with my daughter on how to be in control of yourself.
J. G.

It's important for my family to note the difference in communication. I learned how to react with others, listen, and be more relaxed.
J. N.

I liked getting the information about my mind, body and things to try...stopping to "smell the roses"...will help me be a better dad... It gives you other ways to see things & ways to do them. I think it can help you find yourself in a very positive way.
R. M. D.

This course has shown me that I control my actions and thoughts. I find most helpful to be able to change my habits.It can definitely help your family especially if a family can do this together.
N. R.

I learned to drink water to keep the body hydrated. I learned the info about stress and its effects on the brain. This class helps deal with questions and to have a better awareness of your body.
N. S.

*I knew I would find this program if I would just
keep looking. I wanted this, I needed this.
M. S.*

*The course helps because you need to realize the inner strength.
It is helpful to pay attention to the small things and to share
information with friends and family. It should be taught
to children to free up the thinking process.
S. S.*

*This course has made me know the difference of being so
irritable and thinking too much to just time out and do something
in my life that I like. It was helpful when you told us
about our brain and how our habits can be broken.
L. T.*

*The course gives information on how our brain works and how to relax
and manage our daily stress. The breathing technique
seems to help me the most to relax. I think it would
help when we get angry we could use this technique to calm.
P. W.*

*I can really feel a difference in how I think, and feel sometimes.
It really takes the pressure off, of every day hell in this place.
J. R.*

*A truly positive impact - on dealing with others,
dealing with this place and everyday life.
The breathing technique is wonderful.
Anonymous*

*The principles involved in change...help to move us toward a better
understanding of what we are to what we can be.
Anonymous*

*This class was good for me because I learned some forms and
techniques of relaxing my body in order to have less stress.
It's positive and the Coach teaches
how to avoid problems.
S. A.*

*It is beneficial because you learn the power of your mind.
And that you can live with less stress and pressure.
J. B.*

*The class was useful and at the same time I can teach my family
all that I learned and experienced.
F. C.*

It's always good to learn something positive. It's useful because it helps you to control the bad habits.
J. C.

I gained a different perspective, which helps me with bigger things and to let the small ones go.
M. C.

It helps me think about things in a more positive way. It is a good class especially if you're bad in the street & need to adjust.
R. D.

It has helped me to listen and see both sides of an argument. Waiting five seconds can help you not to rush into things.
C. F.

The class taught me how to make efforts and this important class helped me have better communication with my family.
J. N.

It has taught me how to control my feelings when I am under stress. I have applied my learning on situations where otherwise I could get into fights.
J. O.

It's important to know how to relax and to control your emotions and feelings when you run into problems.
L. O.

By countering negative thought and feelings with positive ones helps relieve daily pressure and depression. I think it would help anyone who tried it.
M. S.

It's good for me and my family to be less angry...to have relaxation and patience. I can resolve problems more calmly.
J. C. V.

Coach Taylor's course helps continually, I'm constantly aware of who I am, and what I need to do.
A. G.

I will do it on a daily basis; to use meditation to handle my lifetime issues that I have had.
C. K.

By applying these techniques, many of the arguments and frustrations can be dealt with better and with less fights.
S. R. M.

By paying attention to my breathing, I can now tell when I am upset and how I can respond appropriately.
J. W.

The course presents life through other eyes and opens your mind. The course helped me alot and I know I can apply what I've learned for long term.
Anonymous

The information presented is useful for dealing with my own feelings, as well as problems that might arise with others. I like the open minded and helpful attitude of the instructor.
Anonymous

It was helpful to have crowd participation, and Interacting or acting out the steps to diffuse stressful situations.
Anonymous

The way to acknowledge a thought that doesn't help me and swap the thought to a positive one was helpful.[You] can't have a heart of stone all the time.
Anonymous

The upbeat positive attitude was helpful...and tips on ways to channel anger. I had a lot of anger before coming here and learned to meditate. This gives me one more tool.
Anonymous

This course is helpful if I stop and think. [Before] if I stopped and thought then I wouldn't be here.
Anonymous

The class helps channel negative energy to positive. Before, I would have taken or done different actions in certain confrontation.
H. M.

The relaxation techniques helped me to sleep better and because of this I didn't wake up as irritable as usual. I believe anything that makes life easier in here can only get better when I'm released.
J. J. C.

The relaxing part and how I learned to concentrate was the most helpful. It helps me when I am lying down on the bunk.
J. G.

I found this class to be great, welcoming and educational. I learned a lot more about the breathing exercises and how to make it habitual.
K. K.

Everyone on this planet can benefit, because Courses like this help us remember that we are all Gods and therefore we are all creators.
M. J.

It helped me at night when I'm in my bunk reading. The most helpful information was the relaxing technique.
J. P.

My perception of life is a lot better. I learned enough here to benefit me in a whole lot of areas in my life. I liked the teacher and the way she answered the inmates' questions.
D. A.

The clear, easy to understand method of [Taylor's] course had a profound effect on my understanding of simple easy to use ways to avoid many problem situations in life. The message compelled me to an awareness of my emotional view of daily life.
J. C.

The Five Second Lightswitch helped me stop smoking. I've learned how to relax and breathe. I will use these techniques for the rest of my life. It's a program that can help me while in the world.
J. B.

On helping children? Love and attention, take the kids out of the hood and show them that there is something else than that hopeless hole.
E. A. C.

It helped me understand other, myself, and the things I need to do to communicate with people...and turn a bad conversation into what I want it to be.
B. B.

I learned how to go after whatever goal you set out to do. And how to relax.
M. B.

I will continue to apply these techniques to help me through my decision process. I understand a pathway to personal change. I feel I learned a great deal.
J. C.

I've learned to channel my shortcomings and stress to where it doesn't bother me anymore. The way you come across, as teacher is excellent. You know how to get your class attention. My only suggestion is that you continue to bless your students with the knowledge you have the same way you have blessed me.
A. C.

By knowing the body and mind and how it works under stress. I learned how to deal with stress, to slow down and be calm.
S. C.

I learned to think positive and to tell yourself that you are ok in all things.
R. C.

Every inmate needs this information on how to manage stress. I've tried it and it works for me. Thank you very much. I will be able to identify my behavior before I act wrongly.
R. E. H.

In general the relaxation I learned helps me clear my mind of anxieties and pave the way to clear thinking. The course is very helpful in everyday management of stress.
P. C.

It taught me a way to set goals and achieve them. I will try to make the information a habit while I'm in here so when I get out it will be embedded.
M. D.

I learned a little more about myself being "fully alive." It's helping me to see things different.
L. R. C.

This course was very informative, the instructor was very easy going and down to earth which helps with communication. It opened my eyes to new ways of dealing with life, people and everyday stuff that life throws at you.
M. E.

I use the breathing technique at night to block out the sounds around me. I learned to think before I do anything.
C. F.

I was helpful to me truly in the relief of stress. Perception, truth and opinion are inter-changeable.
P. C.

Understanding the whole concept and getting to know that other people have the same problems.
R. W. J.

It makes you think and take a look at yourself before pointing the finger.
M. G.

I liked learning to mirror a subject when engaged in dialogue. I've applied the mirror concept during real dialogue with my daughters. The theories on brain functions empathy, mirror neurons, and applying rapport helps in creating open space in the mind, and the environment.
C. G.

The 5-Second Rule really works. I've used it for my diet and it has changed my life...
B. K.

The class helps to stay "focused" on being legit and think before you react.
H. L.

Each day it helps my attitude and I'm insulted by a Negative or threatening inmate, I just turn and walk away.
B. L.

It has been helpful in building confidence in my life, learning to relax, and positive talk.
A. M.

I gave me a center to go to when I have stress. I will apply anchoring, cause & effect and goal setting.
E. P.

I can control a lot of situations better because I think before I act, and I communicate better. I sleep better at night...with less stress.
M. H.

I learned that other peoples' perception is not always reality. And to do what you can do and don't worry.
V. W.

I learned how to change the way I think of myself and how to create an open mind.
J. M.

It has taught me how to communicate better and also be a better person with the people around me, it has helped me how to set goals for myself and reach them.
J.M. L-R.

I find a lot of relief in the simplest concept of this course and that is the breathing techniques. I think that people in this environment build their lives and egos on the wrong principles and this program allows people to focus on self and relearning how to handle simple problems.
J. S.

The instructor is very professional. I like the group experience and the way you teach how to think.
D. M.

This course helped me to practice how to deal with the real world. I'd like to change habits of my loved ones in a positive way by using the class information. I learned how to use natural tools to relax and help me with my sleeping.
A. N.

It will be good when I return home so I can teach my family the things I learned.
D. P.

I believe that the Six Pak Breathing is a real good method...it has really helped me to relax. I shared it with my wife on visit and when she returned she told me how good it makes her feel.
N. R.

for stress also the way the information was brought forth. This is something that everyone can benefit from but, especially inmates because of the dense population. Knowing more about myself and others gives wisdom in all life situations.
M. S.

This course helps anyone at any point in their life - everyday help.
J. S.

This course should be offered to school aged children because it can get them to start off at an earlier age to learn how to deal with themselves on a higher level. The course will continue to help me in my daily life.
S. S.

The class helps to deal with the stress of a changing life. I now have a semi grip on how to recognize and deal with stress.
L. S.

I can apply this information to my whole life. It will help me to deal with different people on any level.
R. F.

Relaxation helps in a lot of different ways, to prepare for a game, to go to sleep, to relieve stress.
Anonymous

I learned to breath myself into a relaxed state from my jaw to my toes......I have settled down a lot.
Anonymous

This course helped me be able to channel my feelings,
deal with obstacles and alleviate some of the tension.
T. T.

Some of us don't have a clue as to how to behave. I learned
how to be confident with whom ever and understand
how important building rapport is.
R. C.

This course makes me help myself. I want to get
a job to take care of my family.
M. F.

The thing I'll remember the most is to drop my hands
and step back! I've learned to deal with things easier.
G. V.

I learned how to deal within a relaxed state of mind and not let
someone's anger dictate my response. I can take
my time thinking things through.
K. H.

All the new perspectives you gave me and the handouts
helped me refer back to and show to friends, in turn
helped me to cement the techniques.
V. N.

I liked the opening of others and participation. The course was helpful
by making me understand in a better way. It opened up many avenues.
M. T.

Any time you're able to learn something new that could be life
sustaining, that's a step towards bettering yourself.
M. E.

I learned how to handle anger in a more productive way. It helps when
encountering people that are hard to deal with in different situations.
D. V.

It really helped me at bedtime to get relaxed and go to sleep at night.
It will help to control my anxiety in tense situations.
V. N.

It will help me to cope with "today" situations. I took this course to be
able to have a place to express some open feelings without being
ridiculed. (It keeps you sane in this environment). I learned how to talk
with my mate and to recognize a problem in her tone of voice.
D. A.

I learned to take power over the conversation and talk from the heart.
It's only me and my mom and we will both improve in the long run.
S. G.

It helped me be more patient. It helped me with talking to my kid's
mother. I will be a better person because of this course.
M. B.

It helped me get a grip on my feelings with my baby's mother. I learned
how to distance my feelings. Relaxation helps me be grounded.
K. B.

She helped me be more responsible and respectful an especially
helped me to work with people as a team. She showed me how to
be a leader, hard worker, and to pay attention,
to listen to suggestions and problems.
R. C.

Relaxation clears my mind and helps me to relieve stress and make
better decisions. It's hard to believe but it brightened my smile.
M. H.

It helped me take a neutral stand on problems that I have no control
over. It helped me not to be judgmental. The course gives
you ideas on how to make changes and improvements.
K. A.

I learned how to breathe in a way I had not knew how.
I learned how to relax and how to breathe and how they both work.
M. B.

[Coach] brings out the inner self. I'm more relaxed on the things I do.
I liked learning to build rapport with people, the way to talk to them.
J. C.

Controlling my breathing helps me relax my body and mind
and soul. It helps me take one day at a time and stay out of trouble.
W. C.

It helped me to re-focus on myself. I cope with things a lot better.
I see things from more than one point of view now.
R. E.

I learned how to relax and actually feel relaxed and well rested after
meditating. When things get too busy and frustrating, I know how to
find relaxation. I liked the different options that I didn't realize I had
because of having a closed mind. I know now when someone
would just want you to listen or just to be there to talk to.
D. F.

It helped me and showed me how to communicate better with my family. I make better decisions now.
J. L. R.

Relaxation helps me relieve stress. I know more ways to have good relationships with people. I will be more mindful now.
A. M.

I learned how to <u>rest</u> better...and how to send messages to the body, my breathing, my brain.
M. R.

I liked that when I was relaxing, I fell asleep. It helped me to concentrate, how to breathe better, and how to control my nerve system.
F. D.

This course helped me relax. I would like to learn more about relaxation, yoga and stretching.
K. V.

The best thing was when I was thinking in my mind about colors and breathing. It is a good feeling to relax.
E. M.

This course helped me learn different breathing steps for relaxing. I liked learning something new about my body.
M. R.

The course helped me understand the way to take pain away from your body. I liked going to sleep and then waking up very relaxed.
Anonymous

I learned that by relaxing, I can help my pains and aches. The course helped me in many ways (everything).
Anonymous

My life is better, being happy and being at peace with others. Relaxation helps me be calm.
Anonymous

I am happier with myself and others. When I'm stressed out and everything is out of control, relaxation helps me by calming down.
J. M. L. R.

It teaches me not to get emotional, to breathe and think before acting. I learned something about myself.
D. A.

*I learned... another strategy on how to deal with my
anger and not have the urge to collapse and use it
for an excuse for my actions.
S. P.*

*Relaxation helps me in not sweating the small stuff
and letting it move on.
V.*

*Thanks for helping me understand the value of life. I will use
all of your teachings to help me when I get out.
B.*

*Coach helped me think different like to stay out of trouble.
And she helped me set goals for myself.
J. A.*

*A coach is a person that teaches people how to run
a good program, help keep kids out of trouble
and lets them know they are a winner.
D. B.*

*The most helpful information of this course
was meditating. It's good to get to know yourself.
T. P.*

*Coach Taylor has helped me because she helps me
value my skills. She has given me new and
better ideas to a new job.
J. G.*

*I learned a lot about methods to reach goals
and cope with my problems...how to prepare
inside for the success in the outside.
A. M.*

*I helped me by showing me how to better communicate with
my family. When I'm stressed out and everything is out of
control the relaxation I learned helps me by calming me down.
J. M. R.*

*I cannot stress enough how Coach Taylor's class has helped me.
She has changed my life and convinced me that I could do anything
I wanted to do with my life despite my record. I like the fact that
you were very supportive, you believed in all of us and helped us
with everything on our minds. And you said constantly
that we could do anything we set our minds to.
M. S.*

Coach Taylor contemplates the GOGI Mission and the goal to reach 1 million individuals in the next few years, empowering them to make positive choices with their lives.

By the way. . .

It is not just my opinion that the current United States of America penal system fails to meet the needs of society. The press, politicians, even guards, probation officers, social workers, judges and police officers will tell you that the current system is not effective. Within a system that does not provide adequate long-term crime prevention, reunification or reentry support, it is almost impossible for an incarcerated individual to realize and act on their inherent goodness. That still does not mean you cannot win! Remember that 30 percent of inmates never return to prison. Why? BECAUSE THEY CHANGE HOW THEY THINK, WHAT THEY SAY, and WHAT THEY DO.

By not addressing the most basic needs of Information, Opportunity and Support, incarceration is often little more than a "warehousing" experience for the more than 2.2 million people in the United States of America behind bars in 2007. High recidivism rates frighten the public. One statistic reports that more than 70 percent of individuals released from prison are re-incarcerated within two years of their release. What is missing is the SELF-empowerment of the inmates. If the system isn't going to help you then you can help yourself. You MUST help yourself if you want to be able to sit and watch a sunset, which is not obscured by razor wire.

Currently, the convict serves his time and may even get time off for good behavior. When he returns to the familiar environment that probably contributed to his incarceration, he is overwhelmed with obstacles such as lack of employment and *financial support. Old friends and old influences and old ways seem to be his only source of support. His decisions are often influenced by his "friends," because this is the only tangible support being offered.*

The People of GOGI

Kids at Hillcrest High School in Inglewood, California, are hard at work, painting the "Wall of Success" as part of a GOGI project.

A majority of society does not believe that a recently released convict is "ready" or "prepared" or "able" to re-enter society and live a crime-free life.

But how is the released individual going to "reunify" when the training, employment, support and opportunities are scarce?

Some in our society perceive all prisoners as evil criminals and best behind bars forever. Others believe prison staffers to be dis-interested government employees or glorified thugs who arbitrarily wield a heavy hand on the disempowered. The staff I meet do not seem to act like bullies or thugs most of the time, although it may seem like they behave that way.

Also, in my experience, the inmates do not act like evil criminals. They may have made bad choices and may have committed hurtful acts against others.

I find that incarcerated men and women are men and women who tried to find respect, food, employment, love, freedom, sanity, or opportunity in illegal ways. Lacking information, opportunity, support, examples and reinforced positive experiences, these individuals do not have an adequate roadmap to success and often follow family footsteps.

I find wardens, guards and prison staffers are employed men and women who sometimes look for respect, food, employment, love, freedom, sanity or opportunity through the power of a uniform, security of a government job, or because their father worked with the Bureau Of Prisons (BOP) and they often follow family footsteps.

Something remarkable happens when I offer respect to both the guards and inmates simultaneously - I meet some amazing prisoners and equally amazing prison guard. Somehow, we all manage to find a collective freedom during our GOGI workshops, if only for an hour at a time.

The Good News is. . .

Many inmates are ready to integrate all available resources available and are willing to learn how to experience their own internal freedom through thought and behavioral change. It does not take much to make a change when you are ready. In truth, our incarceration system does not provide an environment for positive change for a majority of inmates.

The Federal or State government that has confined you is not obligated to help you find yourself. In truth, ninety percent of the individuals in government are imprisoned themselves. They do not have the tools to find their own internal freedom. How can we expect one group of imprisoned individuals to help another group of imprisoned individuals?

This is your personal journey and, with any luck, when you reach your destination of internal freedom you will extend a hand to the guy next to you. We know what internal freedom "looks" like when we see it in the eyes of someone who has reached their destination. There is no specific roadmap. That it is your journey and yours alone.

Those who are released from prison and positively contribute to society are most likely to make internal changes on their own without the "help" of the current penal system.

The GOGI six-week course is currently included in the mandated "Release Preparation Program" at the Federal Correction Institution. It is offered to all incarcerated men within the facility. As of 2007, more than 600 inmates have participated and graduated from the course.

The GOGI tools are or have been taught to at-risk children in Inglewood, Watts and Compton, California, as well as to incarcerated young men through pilot programs designed to help deter crime.

The tools work for men, women, old, young, African Americans, Hispanic, Canadians, Bolivians, Egyptians, Romanians, and all other cultural backgrounds and is not limited to any particular level of education or experience.

The concepts have even been taught to young 5-year-old school children as well as to people in elder care with great results. Regardless of your age, size, shape, gender, religion, education, gang affiliation, crime committed, time left to serve, favorite movie or reading level, you can learn these tools and they can help you find internal freedom.

This book provides tools that have proven to be a catalyst for internal freedom. The tools are universal and easy to remember. They work for anyone, anywhere.

Pass it on. Once you experience internal freedom, I hope you will feel inspired to contribute to the growth and empowerment of other inmates, your family, or friends, and – upon your release – the growth and empowerment of others within your community.

No one has more credibility as a force for positive change than someone who has walked your road. You, too, may be a powerful force for good. They can follow in your footsteps if you choose to share your positive transformation with others.

Acknowledgements and Gratitude

Getting Out by Going In is dedicated to positively influencing lives through the self-empowerment, which results from new information delivered in a supportive environment for a sustained period of time.

My gratitude extends to the adult inmates, as well as their spouses, children and loved ones who participated in the development of the techniques used in this book.

I appreciate the involvement of the incarcerated youth ages 12 - 19 whose participation contributed to the creation of the adolescent and teen version of the GETTING OUT BY GOING IN curriculum.

Without the ongoing permission of the wardens this program might not have been developed. I respectfully express gratitude to the wardens supporting the GOGI program. Many wardens recognize that there are better ways to empower the good in the incarcerated population, than what the system currently employs.

Prison "reform" projects are numerous. Few are able to effect change due to red tape, budgets and the weight of old systems halting their potential. I extend special thanks to the inmates who continue to request the GETTING OUT BY GOING IN program - and to staffers Davis, Torres, O'Brian, Abdul, Richards, Kirkness, and Avery of Federal Corrections Institution (FCI) Terminal Island where this program was born.

I offer my appreciation to the 2004-2005 staff of Camp David Gonzales, Los Angeles County Juvenile Justice Department, and to the boys who willingly participated in the GOGI program. Deputy Parole Officer-Supervisor-MFT-dear friend, Dr. Thomas Kratochvil is an exceptional visionary. Camp Director Eric Ufondu and Jack Sims, supervisors Herbon, Ramirez, and Dela were unwaveringly diligent in supporting "Coach" and the progress they witnessed in the youth who participated.

Pepperdine University's Graduate School of Education and Psychology is appreciated for providing the academic support and the faith in our ability to train future therapists and psychologists in facilitating change.

Pepperdine Professor, Dr. Laurie Scholkopff, inspired the initial volunteer work at FCI Terminal Island. Thanks to Rebecca Reed and Jay Carson for seeing the possibilities. Cathy Kort, Cathleen Cunningham my treasured friends. Joanne McConnell for long distance support.

Thank you to supervisor and valued friend, Melvin M. Moore, for unwavering vision and support. Roselle, I sincerely appreciate you. DeJuan Verrett, you are a man of integrity and dedication to the empowerment of others. Alex Martinez, my love and appreciation. GOGI coaches, you rock. A full heart of appreciation to Tom Melgun, Dave Reichard, Edward LopezLavalle. Jabriel, your art speaks to the soul. Bo and Sita Lozoff you lit the way for me and my work. Charlene Taylor, Richard Taylor and my most treasured friend, Mia Leigh Taylor. Thank you.

These dear friends and supporters understand that we can restructure the current penal system to include the internal freedom and personal empowerment of the incarcerated.

For me, internal freedom came from wanting to be the very best mother I could for my daughter, Mia. Searching for the tools I needed forced me to look inward and accept responsibly for my life. Thank you, Mia, for helping to unlock my internal prison doors.

Most importantly, a very sincere "Thank You" is extended to you, the reader.

The People of GOGI

GOGI Coach Graduation, 2006.

Coach Felicia addresses guests at an appreciation event.

How to Reach GETTING OUT BY GOING IN

This book, and all books published by GETTING OUT BY GOING IN, are supported by donations. The donations provide for the GOGI books to be shipped to any incarcerated individual, free of charge.

Contact GETTING OUT BY GOING IN to request the GOGI books or workbooks to be shipped to you, a friend, or a family member who is incarcerated.

Additionally, you may request information on bringing our programs or speakers to your facility.

If you would like to donate money to provide a book to an incarcerated individual, we would be very grateful.

E-Mail: info@gettingoutbygoingin.org
Website: www.gettingoutbygoingin.org

Address: GETTING OUT BY GOING IN
            PO Box 88969
            Los Angeles, CA 90009 USA

PLEASE HELP US

We rely on your suggestions and your help

Materials in this book were developed with high regard for - *and sincere interest in* - the input and comments of inmates.

Your comments, suggestions and thoughts are valued and may positively influence the lives of others.

Send us your thoughts, your ideas and your experiences so that we might share them with others.

We need your financial support in reaching those who want to change their lives for the better.

GOGI is a non-profit organization. Donations are tax deductible. 501c3 #20-3264893.

PO Box 88969, Los Angeles, CA 90009
www.gettingoutbygoingin.org

GETTING OUT BY GOING IN
YOUR PERSONAL TOOLS FOR INTERNAL FREEDOM

BOSS OF YOUR BRAIN allows you to take control of all your thoughts and actions.

BELLY BREATHING allows you to take control of your entire body.

FIVE SECOND LIGHTSWITCH allow you to stop and think before you act.

WHAT IF? allows you to think from a powerful and positive perspective.

POSITIVE TWA (Thoughts, Words, Actions) TWA are three keys that allows you to control your thoughts, words and actions.

REALITY CHECK allows you to accept the natural process of change.

Name _____ Month _____ Year _____

Certiificate of
Completion

Getting Out
by Going In

GETTING OUT BY GOING IN
PO BOX 88969
Los Angeles, CA 90009, USA

_____
Coach Taylor

Printed in the United States
202877BV00003B/100-1023/A